# 10 STEPS TO STARTING A SMALL AND PROFITABLE BUSINESS

A Journey from Dream to Thriving Reality

## Dick P. Blair

**Copyright © 2024 by Dick P. Blair**

All rights reserved. Before this document is duplicated or reproduce in any manner, the publisher's consent must be gained. Therefore, the contents within can neither be stored electronically, transferred, nor kept in a database. Neither in part nor full can the document be copied, scanned, fixed or retained without approval from the publisher or creator.

# Contents

**Introduction** ..................................................................6

Why Small Business Are More Important Than You May Think ..................................................................................6

**Chapter 1** ....................................................................11

Identify Your Passion and Business Idea.......................11

Generating Concepts for New Businesses ....................13

Evaluating your skills and interests................................15

Realizing Your Business Idea and Validating Your Dream........20

**Chapter 2** ....................................................................25

Conduct Market Research and Validate Your Idea ..............25

Analyzing your competition ..........................................29

Testing your product or service .....................................34

**Chapter 3** ....................................................................39

Develop a Business Plan: Writing your mission statement and goals..................................................................................39

Defining Your Products or Services................................43

Producing a Financial Projection for Your Business Plan ........47

Developing a marketing plan .........................................52

## Chapter 4 .................................................................. 58

Bootstrapping Your Business: Building Your Dreams from the Ground Up .................................................................. 58

Revealing the Finance Scene: Applying for loans or grants .... 61

Crowdfunding Your Entrepreneurial Dreams ........................ 68

## Chapter 5 .................................................................. 73

Selecting the Right Business Structure for Your Entrepreneurial Journey ........................................................ 73

Bringing Your Idea to Life: Registering Your Business with the Government.................................................................... 77

Getting Through the Maze: Obtaining the Necessary Licenses and Permits for Your Business ................................................ 82

## Chapter 6 .................................................................. 88

Create a Marketing Plan and Build Your Brand: Establishing Your Brand in a Competitive Environment ............................. 88

Developing Effective Marketing Strategies to Propel Your Brand ................................................................................ 92

Weaving the Web: Orchestrating Online and Offline Marketing Channels for Brand Harmony ................................................ 97

## Chapter 7 .................................................................. 103

From Vision to Validation: Creating Prototypes and Minimum Viable Products (MVPs) ........................................................ 103

Finding Reliable Suppliers and Vendors for Your Business ...107

Ensuring Quality Control in Your Products or Services .........112

## Chapter 8 ................................................................................117

Launch Your Business and Start Selling: Setting your launch date and creating a buzz ......................................................117

Implementing Your Marketing Plan for Launch Success .......121

Making your first sales: Strategies and Tactics to Secure Your Initial Customers ...............................................................126

## Chapter 9 ................................................................................132

Keeping Accurate Financial Records for Business Success ...132

Analyzing Your Sales and Marketing Data for Growth ..........136

Making Adjustments to Your Business Plan for Sustainable Growth ...............................................................................141

## Chapter 10 ..............................................................................147

The Road to Success: Overcoming Common Challenges Faced by Small Businesses .........................................................147

Overcoming Obstacles: Strategies for Sustainable Business Growth ...............................................................................151

Crucial Tools for Successful Small Business Ventures ..........155

# Introduction

*Why Small Business Are More Important Than You May Think*

Have you ever wondered what makes the little coffee shop on the block seem so unique? Or why is there so much life and energy at the neighborhood farmers market? It's about the influence small companies make on our lives, not simply about the colorful veggies or the tasty cappuccino.

Here's a quick glimpse into why they're so important:

1. Job creators: Small enterprises are the true job generators; forget about large multinationals! They create chances for individuals in communities all around the world, making up the overwhelming bulk of newly created employment. That charming bakery across the street may thus be your neighbor's key to stable finances.
2. Innovation powerhouses: Small enterprises have a tenacious spirit that should not be undervalued! They frequently serve as hubs for creativity, continuously producing fresh concepts and solutions. Do you recall your town's first organic food store? Or the local coffee shop that ignited the kombucha

trend? Yes, there were probably little companies making waves in the market.
3. Cornerstones of the community: Small businesses are the lifeblood of our communities; they are more than just locations to shop. They support charitable organizations, organize neighborhood activities, and offer a welcoming face when you need it. That sense of acceptance you receive from your favorite bookshop? That embodies the strength of small enterprises.
4. Diverse opinions, varied options: Are you sick of the same old thing? Small companies provide a welcome change of pace. They offer a wide variety of goods and services, celebrate distinctive cultures, and cater to specialized consumers. In other words, chances are a tiny firm can provide what you're searching for.

But before you jump headfirst into the exciting world of entrepreneurship, **let's talk about what it really takes to be a successful one.**

Are You Prepared for the Courage and Grit of Entrepreneurship?

It may seem wonderful to be your own boss, but let's be honest—things aren't always sunshine and rainbows. A preview of what to expect is provided here:

- Your passion is your fuel: Starting a business is a journey, not a sprint. Having enthusiasm for your concept is essential to persevere despite the inevitable obstacles. It's the fire that propels you to grow, change, and get over challenges.

- Put on numerous hats (and learn how to juggle): You'll be handling a variety of responsibilities in your small business, from finance wizard to marketing master. Be ready to take on new responsibilities, pick up new skills, and accept how the world of entrepreneurship is always evolving.
- Resilience is your superpower. It is unavoidable. But resilience is the secret to success. You'll need to keep moving forward with a good mindset, learn from your mistakes, and recover from setbacks.
- Community is your lifeline: No businessperson is an island. It is essential to surround oneself with a network of mentors, advisers, and other small company owners who will help you. They will encourage you when you succeed, support you when things become hard, and let you know you're not traveling this path alone.
- Patience is Key: It takes time to establish a profitable business. Don't count on success right now. Have faith in the process, be patient, and acknowledge tiny accomplishments. The benefits of creating anything from scratch are definitely worth the time investment.

Are you prepared to take the call now? If the response is a resounding "yes," **let's discuss the important factors to take into account before making the decision.**

## Before You Dive In: Essential Considerations

It's a thrilling journey to launch a business, but planning is key. Prior to taking action, think about these crucial questions: How much money do you have? Regarding the amount of money you have to invest, be reasonable and look into funding sources. Remember that even the most brilliant ideas require a strong financial basis.

Do you know anything about the industry? Power comes from knowledge! Investigate your intended audience, comprehend your rivals, and keep up with market developments.

Is your business plan well-defined? A thorough strategy that outlines your objectives, tactics, and financial predictions is the first step on your road map to prosperity.

What are your responsibilities under law and regulation? It might be challenging to navigate legal and regulatory constraints. Seek expert counsel to make sure your company complies with the law.

Are you ready to make the personal sacrifice? Managing a business demands commitment, diligence, and selflessness.

Regarding the amount of time and effort you're willing to put in, be truthful with yourself.

Remember that launching a small business is an individual endeavor. It's about pursuing your goals, changing the world, and giving back to your neighborhood. With meticulous preparation, unshakable devotion, and a network of allies.

# Chapter 1

*Identify Your Passion and Business Idea*

In reality, what should you do with your life? Finding the sweet spot where your talents and interests meet your passion is the first step towards launching a modest but lucrative business. Let's get intimate for a moment; forget about spreadsheets and market data!

Consider what motivates you. What skills come easily to you? Which are the hobbies that lead you to lose track of time since you're having so much fun? Do you enjoy working with technology, crafting moving tales, creating mouthwatering meals, or planning happy occasions for others? Finding a business concept that fulfills your spirit requires first identifying your own abilities and interests.

But passion on its own is insufficient. It's like having a tasty recipe that is simply words on paper if the proper elements aren't added. That's where your expertise and abilities are useful. Do you have the ability to create websites without any guidance? A master writer capable of creating magic out of promotional copy? A gregarious butterfly with the ability to establish long-lasting connections with anyone? Finding business ideas that capitalize on your abilities and reduce the learning curve is made easier by identifying your current competencies and areas of competence.

Let's get inventive now! Think creatively as if there is no tomorrow. In novel ways, combine your talents and hobbies. Could a bespoke cookie decorating company with inspirational messages arise from your passion for baking and your skill at telling stories? Or perhaps you were inspired to develop a cutting-edge music instruction software by your love of music and your technological prowess?

Note that most of the greatest business concepts address a problem. Examine your surroundings and identify any gaps in your neighborhood or the global community. Is a more environmentally friendly clothing line necessary? A website that links dog walkers in the area with pet owners? A professional decluttering service for busy people' homes and minds?

Don't be scared to try new things! The ability to test and iterate is one of the best things about beginning small. Create a prototype, take on a side project, or charge for your skills. Observe how others respond, get input, and hone your concept in light of practical experiences.

Discovering the business idea concept is a process rather than a final goal. Accept the process of discovery, follow your instincts, and don't be scared to get dirty. Remember that the most prosperous business are frequently those that are founded on a solid foundation of enthusiasm, meaning, and a sincere desire to change the world. Go forth, pursue your interests, and come up with the company concept that lights your spirit on fire!

## Generating Concepts for New Businesses

Now is the moment to let your inner businessperson go! The process of generating business ideas through brainstorming is the initial stage towards transforming your idea into a successful enterprise. It can also be a lot of fun. Instead of using dull lists, let's explore some original methods to spark your creativity:

1. Mind Mapping Madness: Take out a large piece of paper or use a mind mapping application, then just let your thoughts roam. Your hobbies, abilities, and interests should come first. Then, expand outside with ideas that are linked to them, issues you observe, and potential solutions. Just write everything down without passing judgment! Where the links go, you would not expect.

2. Shower Power: Have you ever seen how inspiration often strikes when shampooing? That's because of something! The shower's calm, judgment-free atmosphere is ideal for inspiring creative thought processes in your subconscious. So the next time you're sudsing up, grab a waterproof paper or mentally scribble down anything that comes to mind.
3. Issue Investigator: Don your Sherlock Holmes cap and take on the role of a problem investigator! Examine your neighborhood, online discussion boards, or even your own life to see what's lacking, annoying, or just inconvenient. Is there any way you can use a product, service, or original idea to tackle those issues?
4. Borrow and Blend: Don't be scared to incorporate ideas from other companies into your own ventures! Consider combining two unconnected ideas to create something new. Imagine a dog walking business that provides a percentage of its profits to animal shelters, or a yoga class that doubles as a coffee store.
5. Collaboration Chaos: Get together with your loved ones, friends, or even online groups of people who share similar interests and histories. Give the groupthink a problem or brainstorming stimulus, and see what wild, amazing ideas come to life. The more varied the viewpoints, the more original and surprising the ideas might be!

6. Get Out and Explore: Occasionally, venturing beyond your comfort zone may provide the most inspiring ideas. Go to regional markets, go to business gatherings, or simply strike up a discussion with a complete stranger. You never know what can spark the idea for your next major project.

To have a fruitful brainstorming session, always remember to think creatively, accept unconventional ideas, and quiet your inner critic. Many of the most prosperous companies began with apparently absurd ideas, so don't be scared to dream large and enjoy the process!

## Evaluating your skills and interests

Starting a business is an incredible adventure, but with endless possibilities, it can often feel overwhelming. What is the best way to decide which way to go? Where do you even begin? The answer lies within – unlocking your passions, understanding your skills, and letting them guide you towards a fulfilling business idea.

In this in-depth analysis, we'll look at how self-evaluation may be a useful tool for finding a business idea that not only has the potential to succeed but also gives you a true sense of fulfillment and purpose. It's time to find the hidden talents within you that will ignite your entrepreneurial endeavors!

## 1. Harness the Power of Passion

Imagine having a true love for what you do and looking forward to taking on the difficulties of your business each day rather than just doing it out of obligation. That is the force of enthusiasm! It's the strength that will carry you through difficult times and the voice inside that says, "This is worth it."

The following activities can assist you in discovering your passions:

- The Childhood Curiosity Test: Recall the carefree times when you were absorbed in a task and time seemed to stand still. What activity did you enjoy? Was it constructing elaborate Lego models? Composing tales set on imaginary realms? Putting the pantry in order with extreme precision? Our deeper passions are frequently shown via the interests we had as children.
- The "I Would Do This For Free" Challenge: Make a list of all the tasks you frequently perform even without compensation. Do you enjoy making lovely spreadsheets for friends, spending hours editing movies for them, or mediating disputes amongst people? These pursuits probably appeal to your innate drives and interests.
- Follow Your Energy: Pay attention to when you feel the most engaged and enthusiastic throughout the day. Which

tasks give you a sense of excitement and life? Conversely, what depletes you and makes you feel disinterested or uninspired? Knowing how your energy flows will help you identify your genuine passions.

Note that passion encompasses more than simply enjoyable pastimes. It all comes down to a strong sense of purpose, a strong bond with the task, and a conviction in its importance.

## 2. Understanding the Power of Your Skills

While talents are the means by which you transform your passion into a long-term business, passion serves as the fuel. It's critical to evaluate your abilities honestly and consider how they may be turned into offers that the market will buy in order to make sure your business survives.

Let's break down your skills into three categories:

1. Hard skills: are your technical prowess, which you may quantify and validate with credentials or prior work experience. Several trade skills, foreign languages, graphic design, coding, bookkeeping, event organizing, and copywriting are a few examples.
2. Soft skills: are the transferable and interpersonal abilities that enable you to work well with others, solve problems on the fly, and persuade others. Leadership, critical

thinking, negotiation, empathy, time management, and conflict resolution are a few examples.
3. Hidden Skills: These are the abilities you may take for granted, the "obvious" talents at which you naturally shine. Maybe you're a terrific networker, a born organizer, or you just have a magical way of making people laugh. Never undervalue these seemingly easy skills!

## 3. Conduct a Skill Audit

It's time to get your hands dirty and assess your abilities. Here's a productive method to get things done:

- List It All Out: Take Out Your Notepad and Begin Enumerating All Your Skills, No Matter How Small. Include any abilities you have developed from hobbies, volunteer work, or life experiences; don't only focus on your job experience.
- Collect Evidence: Jot down concrete instances of your use of each skill. This might include prior undertakings, successes, endorsements, or even anecdotal evidence. Evidence gives you confidence and supports your abilities.
- Seek Outside Input: Occasionally, we fail to see our own advantages. To determine your greatest abilities, ask mentors, friends, family, and past coworkers. Their insights may astound you and reveal untapped abilities.

## Combining Everything: Locating the Sweet Spot

It's time for some creative thinking now that you have a firm grasp on your interests and abilities! Seek out the spaces where these two components meet. Where does your heart shine brightest, and where do you possess the skills to support your zeal?

Here are some thought-provoking questions to guide you:

- What issues do you find exciting and frustrating in the world today? Are there any issues that you firmly feel need to be resolved, and may your interests and abilities help?
- What is it that you usually assist people with? Do people come to you for life coaching, fashion guidance, or tech help on a regular basis? These innate areas of competence might be the secret to a successful commercial endeavor.
- Are you able to creatively blend your interests and abilities? Maybe you combine your passion for graphic design with your love of animals to make custom pet pictures. Alternatively, you might use your love of healthy living and your aptitude for organizing to provide meal prep services.
- Never be scared to think creatively! The most inventive business idea frequently result from strange pairings.

Allow your creativity to flow and investigate how your special combination of interests and abilities may result in a genuinely distinctive service.

## Realizing Your Business Idea and Validating Your Dream

You now have a blazing passion and a wonderful business idea simmering away in the back of your head. That's quite impressive! Validating your idea is an essential step to do before you commit all of your time and money.

Imagine devoting your entire being to starting a business, only to learn afterwards that your target market isn't interested in what you have to offer. You may reduce the likelihood of failure and improve your chances of creating a long-lasting, profitable company that genuinely fills a need by taking the time to verify your idea.

So, how can you use a market fit to turn your fascinating concept from a pipe dream into a reality?

### Step 1: Identify Who Your Target Market Is
Knowing who you are aiming to target is the first step towards validating your concept. Who will be the perfect client for you?

What are their goals, desires, problems, and needs? This clarity enables you to craft a message and offer that will truly speak to them.

This is how to begin:

- Perform Market Research: To learn about the latest trends, search terms, and conversations in your area, use internet resources such as Google Trends and social media listening platforms.
- Make Buyer Personas: Describe your ideal client in great depth, including their buying patterns, psychographics, and difficulties.
- Speak with Prospective Clients: Survey or interview prospective clients in your intended market. Inquire about their preferences, issues, and existing methods for resolving these difficulties. This candid criticism is really helpful.

**Step 2: Examine the Rivals**

No company can function in a vacuum. It is important that you comprehend the identities, products, and market positioning of your rivals. With this information, you can see possible holes and chances to differentiate your own company.

Here's how to evaluate your rivals:

- Determine Who Your Primary Rivals Are: What companies currently provide comparable goods or services to your intended market?
- Examine Their Offerings: What Are The Advantages and Disadvantages? What are their marketing tactics and pricing policies?
- Find Differentiation Opportunities: What special and worthwhile offering can you make that your rivals cannot?

**Step 3: Conduct Pre-Launch Validation to Test the Waters**
Don't hold off on sharing your concept until everything is ideal. You may get input and improve your idea through pre-launch validation before investing a lot of money.

A few pre-launch validation techniques are as follows:

- The Minimum Viable Product (MVP): is a rudimentary form of your good or service that has only enough functionality to prove its worth and elicit input from users.
- Test Your Landing Page: Create a landing page that explains your company idea and provides a mechanism for prospective clients to show interest, place a preorder, or subscribe to updates. This measures the reaction of the audience and future demand.

- Social Media Engagement: Post your concept on sites like Facebook or Twitter, start discussions, and observe the responses you receive. Interact with remarks and inquiries to learn about the wants and worries of possible clients.

**Step 4: Examine the Feedback Loop**

Pre-launch validation is beautiful because of the feedback loop it generates. Through gathering information and input from your market analysis, interviews, and pre-launch events, you may better understand whether your company concept will succeed.

Here's how to analyze the feedback:

- Determine trends and patterns: Analyze the input you get for any reoccurring themes. Are there any particular issues that require attention? Is there a constant interest in what you have to offer?
- Be willing to change course: Don't be scared to modify your plan in response to criticism. Developing a product or service that genuinely appeals to your target market is the aim, and sometimes it requires being adaptable and changing your original plan.
- Put an emphasis on practical insights: Don't only gather information; utilize it to guide your judgments. Make any

adjustments to your offering in light of feedback, and make sure you take into account the requirements and worries expressed by prospective clients.

Take note that the process of validation is continuous. Continue to get client input as your firm develops and grows to make sure you stay current and can adjust to the demands of the market.

By adhering to these guidelines and accepting the iterative validation process, you may raise the likelihood that your company concept will materialize into a prosperous enterprise. Never forget that even the best concepts must be tried, improved, and adjusted to fit the demands of your target audience. Thus, affirm, adjust, and watch as your business aspirations soar!

Note: Don't let your fear of failing immobilize you, even though validation is important. Accept the process of development and learning. Even if you have to change or rework your original idea from the insightful knowledge you obtain from

# Chapter 2

*Conduct Market Research and Validate Your Idea*

Your business idea is like a seed full of promise when you're an entrepreneur. However, it needs fertile ground—a target market that appreciates what you have to give and connects with your offering—before it can take off and become a profitable endeavor.

Discovering the essence of your ideal client is just as important to understanding your target market as learning about their demographics. It's about understanding their requirements, desires, goals, and even areas of discomfort. This thorough comprehension is essential for doing fruitful market research and, eventually, for validating your company concept.

So, how do you truly understand the pulse of your target market?

**Step 1: create a persona for your audience.**
Creating a consumer persona is essential before doing any market research. This is a comprehensive profile of your

prospective customer that goes beyond their geography and age. It explores their:
- Demographics: location, age, gender, economic bracket, and degree of education.
- Psychographics: Online behavior, personality traits, interests, values, and lifestyle decisions.
- Needs and Pain Points: What difficulties do they face? What issues need to be resolved for them?
- Buying Habits: What methods do people use to investigate and buy goods and services? Which channels do they favor, and what variables influence their decisions?

**Creating an engaging buyer persona may be accomplished by:**
- Market research data: To learn more about your target market, use consumer surveys, industry studies, and market analysis tools.
- Competition analysis: To obtain a more comprehensive picture of the market environment, examine the target market and message of your rivals.
- Customer interviews and surveys: Use focus groups, surveys, and interviews to gain direct information about the requirements and preferences of your target market.

**Step 2: Set Out to Conduct Market Research**

It's time to compile both quantitative and qualitative information on your target market after you have a clear image of your perfect client. This will assist you in determining the viability of your business concept and guarantee that it genuinely meets their demands.

The following is a toolkit of market research techniques:

- Secondary Research: Make use of easily accessible data from industry journals, government organizations, and research businesses. This provides insightful information on market size, trends, and competitive landscape.
- Surveys & Questionnaires: Create online or offline surveys to gather information from a sizable portion of your intended market. This assists in determining their level of awareness of your service, gathering feedback, and estimating possible interest.
- Social Listening: To get insight into online discussions, patterns, and user-generated material associated with your sector and specialty, employ social media listening systems. This provides insightful information about their needs, interests, and problems.
- Focus groups: Have in-depth conversations about your company concept and its offerings with a small group of

people that make up your target audience. Find out about their attitudes, views, and impressions.
- Interviews with customers: Arrange private, one-on-one conversations with specific members of your target market to learn more about their attitudes, drives, and decision-making procedures.

## Step 3: Examine and Explain Your Results

It's time to evaluate and understand the data from your market research after you've collected it. This is where the magic happens: it transforms unprocessed data into insights that can be used to inform business choices.

The following are some crucial points to consider:

- Identify trends and patterns: Find reoccurring themes and patterns in your data to help you identify trends and patterns. What wants, difficulties, and preferences does your target audience frequently express?
- Market segmentation: Determine possible sub-segments within your target market based on your study. This enables you to customize your services and messaging to meet the diverse requirements and tastes of the larger audience.

- Verify your idea: Did your study confirm the market demand you first anticipated for your company idea? Do you need to make any changes or alterations to better connect with your target audience?

**Step 4: Accept Refinement and Iteration**
Remember that conducting market research is an ongoing process. It is a continuous procedure. Review your study results and revise your perception of your target market as your business grows and the market environment shifts.

Be ready to adjust your messaging and offering in light of fresh information. By using an iterative strategy, you can make sure that your business stays current and resonates with your target audience, which will eventually lead to long-term success.

Knowing your target market allows you to Create a good or service that really meets their wants.

Create persuasive, engaging marketing messaging that are specifically targeted. Create sincere connections with your clients to encourage advocacy and loyalty.

Remember that prosperous companies aren't created overnight. They are based on a thorough grasp of their customers. By putting in the time and effort to fully comprehend the target market.

# Analyzing your competition

Entering the business world as an entrepreneur may be likened to walking into a coliseum, full of driven rivals fighting for the same clientele. It is important to have a thorough awareness of your rivals' strengths and shortcomings in order to identify any possible holes in the market and strategically position your own organization. Analyzing your competition is a thought-provoking process that can help you start and expand sustainably, much like figuring out a strategic blueprint.

## Step 1: Determine Who Your Main Rivals Are

Finding your main competitors in the market is the first stage in the competitive analysis process. This is more than merely acknowledging the well-known businesses. Seek out companies who cater to your target demographic with comparable goods or services, even if they are in a somewhat different market or employ different advertising techniques.

Here are a few techniques to determine who your main rivals are:

- Market research reports: To learn more about your business and discover key players, consult industry studies and publications.
- Internet searches: Use pertinent terms and phrases from your business and target market when conducting internet

searches. This will highlight well-known brands and possible niche rivals.
- Customer interviews and surveys: Inquire about the brands and companies that your target market currently uses for comparable goods and services from your target audience during market research.

## Step 2: Deconstructing the Competition: Strengths and Weaknesses

It's time to delve deeply into your competitors' business tactics when you have a list of your main rivals. Examine their:
- Goods and Services: What do they provide, and how do theirs and yours compare in terms of features, cost, and value?
- Marketing and Sales Strategies: How can marketing and sales strategies persuade their intended audience to notice them? Which channels do they use for marketing?
- Pricing Strategies: How do they set the pricing for their goods and services? What elements appear to have an impact on their price choices?
- Customer Service: How well-known is their customer service department? How do they respond to questions and grievances from clients?
- Strengths and Weaknesses: Based on your study, list their main advantages and disadvantages. Why are they doing

so well, exactly? Where do they appear to be weak points or gaps?

To keep informed about the most recent announcements, initiatives, and consumer sentiment from your rivals, make use of internet resources like as industry journals and social media listening services.

**Step 3: Finding Possibilities in the Market**

Through a thorough examination of your rivals' advantages and disadvantages, you might spot possible business prospects. These chances might include:

- Supplying a special feature or service that is absent from your rivals.
- Focusing on a certain clientele that hasn't yet been reached by your rivals.
- Creating a more economical or efficient delivery method for your service.
- Utilizing an alternative marketing channel to successfully reach your target market.

**Step 4: Differentiate and Position Your Business**

Gaining a firm foothold in the market and differentiating your company from the competition requires an understanding of your rivals. You may draw in and keep clients by emphasizing your special selling point and fixing the flaws of your rivals.

Here's how to differentiate your business:
- Concentrate on your USP, or unique selling proposition, which is what makes you stand out from the competition. For your intended audience, what distinguishes and adds value to your offering?
- Highlight your advantages: Use your special skills and resources to meet the demands of your target market in a manner that your rivals cannot.
- Explain your value proposition to your target audience in a clear and engaging way by creating a message that does just that.

Always put in mind that the goal of studying your rivals is to gain knowledge from them, not to emulate them. Through comprehension of their tactics, advantages, and disadvantages, you may proactively arrange your enterprise for long-term expansion and prosperity.

Working together with non-direct rivals in your sector shouldn't scare you. Your reach and effect may be increased through strategic alliances, which can provide you access to new markets, resources, and consumer groups.

You can confidently traverse the competitive landscape by mastering the art of competitive intelligence. Note that knowing your competitors gives you the ability to forge your own route, draw in your target clients, and create a successful company that stands out from the competition.

## Testing your product or service

You've determined your fervent mission, explored your target market in great detail, and even examined the competition environment. The real test is about to begin: putting your product or service through its paces to make sure it meets the needs of your target market and verify your idea. This stage is critical to converting your idea from a viable concept into a successful, customer-focused product. It involves getting insightful, practical feedback from your target market so you can improve your concept, spot possible roadblocks, and eventually introduce a good or service that really fulfills their requirements and goes above and beyond.

**Step 1: Selecting Your Method of Testing**
There isn't a single, universal strategy for testing products or services. The best approach may vary depending on your resources, product/service type, and development stage.

Here are a few well-liked testing techniques:
- A minimal viable product (MVP): is a working, functioning version of your product or service that has the essential functionality needed to highlight its main selling point and elicit input from customers. By releasing an MVP, you can swiftly iterate based on user insights, test essential features, and get early feedback.
- Prototyping: Making a low-fidelity or non-functional prototype of your product or service is known as prototyping. Prototypes are useful for obtaining early input on the user experience, design, and general concept. They can be digital or physical.
- A/B Testing: compares two variations of your product or service (e.g., features, pricing structures, or advertising copy) to determine which version appeals to your target market the most.
- User Interviews and Focus Groups: Focus groups and user interviews are participatory methods that let you get detailed input straight from prospective consumers. Get insightful information about their wants, perspectives, and possible pain spots by seeing how they engage with your product/service prototype and by asking open-ended questions.
- Beta Testing: A limited version of your product or service is released to a select set of early adopters as part of beta

testing. Prior to a wider release, beta testers offer insightful input on functionality, user experience, and general market fit.

## Step 2: Find Subjects for Your Test Group

It's important to find the correct people to test your service or product. A varied cross-section of your target market should ideally be represented in your test group. This guarantees that you get input from people with different requirements, tastes, and viewpoints.

Here are a few strategies for assembling your test group:
- Social media: To contact the perfect client profile and ask them to take part in testing, use focused social media campaigns.
- Online communities: Participate in relevant online forums and communities that are associated with your business or specialty. Provide rewards for involvement and solicit insightful input from prospective consumers.
- Customer list: Make the most of your current clientele if you have one! Give them early access to your offering in return for their opinions.

## Step 3: Conducting the Test and Gathering Feedback

It's time to administer the exam and get feedback after you've selected your testing strategy and gathered your test group. These are important things to keep in mind:

- Set clear objectives: Clearly define your goals for this testing phase and what you hope to learn from it. What particular queries do you need answered? Which features of your offering—product or service—are you most eager to hear about from customers?
- Establish a user-friendly testing environment: By making sure the procedure is unambiguous, simple to follow, and doesn't deter participation.
- Observe and gather feedback: Pay attention to how customers engage with your offering and proactively invite them to share their thoughts via open-ended questions, interviews, and surveys.
- Be open to criticism: Don't take criticism personally. See it as a chance to gain knowledge and enhance your offering.

## Step 4: Examine and Modify Your Concept

It's time to examine the facts and modify your idea in light of the new understandings you've received after receiving input from your test group. The real magic of testing occurs at this point. Seek out:

- Recurring themes and patterns: Do customers consistently encounter problems or difficulties when utilizing your product or service?
- Positive and negative comments: Which features of your product appeal to users? What is in need of improvement?
- Possibilities for innovation: In light of the comments, are there any innovations or upgrades that may improve your offering?
- Accept the iterative process: Don't be scared to make changes to your offering in response to customer input. By using an iterative strategy, you can make sure that your product keeps changing to suit the demands and preferences of your target market.

# Chapter 3

*Develop a Business Plan: Writing your mission statement and goals*

You've taken a critical step in validating your business concept by conducting market research and testing, and it seems like a winning venture. It's time to turn your idea into a concise, workable business plan at this point. This document serves as your road map, directing your choices, drawing in possible backers, and guaranteeing that your business endeavors remain on course.

Your mission statement and goals are two essential components that provide the groundwork for success in the business plan. Let's examine how to create these effective tools that will advance your company.

## 1. How to Define Your Mission Statement: The Heart of Your Business

A mission statement isn't merely a memorable tagline. Your company's primary goal is what gives it direction and establishes its existence. It encapsulates your business's core principles, goals, and intended global influence.

When creating your mission statement, keep the following important components in mind:

- **Who are you?** Give a brief overview of your business and its main products.
- **What makes you unique?** Emphasize what makes your business unique compared to its rivals.
- **What benefit do you offer?** Describe the ways in which your company helps the community and its clients.
- **What is your impact?** Describe the wider influence that your company initiatives are intended to achieve.

Here are a few motivational mission statement examples:

- **Google's** mission is "To organize the world's information and make it universally accessible and useful."
- **Patagonia** says, "Build the best product, cause no unnecessary harm, use business to inspire and implement solutions to the environmental crisis."
- **TOMS** stands for "One for One®. With every product you purchase, TOMS will provide a new pair of shoes to a child in need."

Keep in mind that your mission statement ought to be succinct, understandable, and unambiguous. It should strike a chord with your intended audience and motivate your group to meet your objectives.

## 2. Defining Objectives: Creating a Successful Course

It's time to turn your mission statement into attainable objectives after you've established it. These objectives act as your road signs, pointing you in the direction of realizing your overarching vision.

The following are some crucial components of successful goal-setting:
- Make sure your objectives are Time-bound, Relevant, Specific, Measurable, and Achievable (SMART) goals. This structure makes everything clear and makes goal monitoring easier.
- Establish a balance between short-term objectives that commemorate accomplishments and long-term objectives that keep an eye on the wider picture.
- Aligned with your mission: Your objectives have to be in direct relation to and enhance your mission statement as a whole.

Here are some examples of setting goals based on your mission statement:

- Mission Statement: "To provide exceptional customer service and build long-lasting relationships with our clients."
- Goal 1 (short-term): In the upcoming quarter, reach a 95% customer satisfaction rating.
- Goal 2 (Long-term): Within the following year, increase participation in the customer loyalty program by 20%.

Keep an eye on and adjust your goals all the time. Be ready to modify your goals as your company grows and the market conditions shift in order to stay focused on accomplishing your purpose.

**Above and beyond the words:**

Understand that your objectives and mission statement are more than simply words on a page. These are dynamic papers that capture the essential principles and goals of your company. You can give your team direction, draw in investors who share your vision, and eventually create the conditions for long-term, significant success by developing a compelling mission statement and creating SMART goals.

Talk about your goals and mission statement with your partners, customers, and staff without fear. This openness inspires everyone to work together to realize your goal and creates a feeling of shared purpose.

You can create a compelling mission statement and set goals that will drive your company ahead by following these steps and embracing constant learning. This will guarantee that your entrepreneurial path is both worthwhile and prosperous.

## Defining Your Products or Services

Similar to a blueprint, your business plan serves as a thorough road map to help you navigate the thrilling but difficult world of entrepreneurship. A key component of this strategy is identifying your products or services, which serves as the foundation for your whole enterprise. This part serves as a portal into the heart of your business, presenting your offerings and how they meet the demands of your intended market.

That being said, how can you properly and informatively define your products or services? Fasten your seatbelts, as we're about to explore the realm of offers!

### 1. Delving into the Details: What Makes You Tick?

Before you write a compelling description, thoroughly examine the core of what you have to offer. Consider the following inquiries for yourself:

- What are you selling? Whether it's a digital service like a language learning program or a physical commodity like handcrafted jewelry, clearly identify your offerings.
- What makes them unique? Determine what makes your products or services stand out from the crowd. Does your baking mix contain a unique ingredient, or does your fitness program provide one-on-one coaching that can't be found anywhere else? Drawing attention to your unique selling point (USP) is essential.
- Which particular issues do you resolve? Clearly state the needs or pain areas that your services are meant to alleviate. Do the garments you make by hand fit a particular fashion niche that is hard to fill with mass-produced alternatives? Or does your accounting software provide functions that make things easier for small firms to accomplish? To draw in the ideal clients, it's important to comprehend the issue you resolve.
- How do you help the people you want to reach? Don't just list the features. Describe the advantages your offerings give, both material and immaterial. Does your meal prep service encourage wholesome eating habits while saving clients money and time? Or does your pet grooming service provide pets and their owners with a stress-free experience in addition to clean fur?

## 2. Write a Captivating Description: Painting a Picture with Words

Now that you have a solid understanding of your offerings, it's time to craft a compelling description that captures the essence and value proposition. Here are some key elements to consider:

- Clarity and conciseness: Speak in a way that your target audience may easily comprehend by using language that is clear and concise. Steer clear of acronyms and technical language that might mislead potential clients.
- Feature-focused: Pay attention to the advantages your products or services offer, not just their features. Recall that consumers purchase solutions, not simply goods or services, to solve their issues.
- Emotional connection: To connect with your audience on an emotional level, incorporate a hint of emotion. In what ways will your products and services improve, simplify, or enhance their lives?
- Actionable language: Use language that is actionable to nudge readers toward the next action. Make an effort to persuade them to contact you, learn more, or perhaps make a purchase by using persuasive language.

## 3. Introducing Your Products: Inexpressible

Though a well-written description is crucial, think about adding images to further highlight what you have to offer. Here are a few choices:

- High-quality images: Provide eye-catching pictures or films that demonstrate your items in action while graphically emphasizing their features and advantages.
- Interactive components: To provide prospective buyers a more engaging experience, think about integrating interactive components like 360° product views or demo films.
- Case studies and customer testimonials: To establish credibility and trust, share true tales and endorsements from contented clients.

**4. Remember, that this is a continuous process.**

Clearly defining your goods or services is a continuous process. Your product descriptions should change as your business does. Be ready to modify and improve them in response to client demands, market input, and your overarching business plan.

By precisely outlining, summarizing, and presenting your products, you not only educate prospective clients but also reinforce your own perception of what makes your business special and worthwhile. This clarity serves as the cornerstone for your marketing initiatives, helping you draw in the proper clientele and establish a profitable business.

So, let your imagination go wild, dive into the core of what you have to offer, and use words to create a visual representation of what makes your business genuinely unique!

## Producing a Financial Projection for Your Business Plan

Your business plan is like a map that points the way to success for your entrepreneurial endeavors. The financial projection is a key component of this important document. It functions like a crystal ball, providing an insight into the anticipated financial well-being of your business. This prediction is a useful tool for understanding your financial viability as well as for obtaining investments, making financial decisions, and making sure your business succeeds in the long term.

**Step 1: Understanding the Purpose of a Financial Forecast**
Prior to getting too technical, it's important to comprehend why a financial projection is made:

- Planning and Goal-Setting: It aids in the establishment of milestones, the setting of reasonable financial targets, and the evaluation of whether your company model is profitable.
- Making Decisions: You can decide wisely on investments, pricing policies, and resource allocation by having a solid grasp of your anticipated income, costs, and cash flow.
- Investment & funds: Attracting investors and obtaining funds require a clear financial projection. It shows that you are aware of the financial environment and have the skills necessary to run the company efficiently.
- Performance Monitoring: You may track your actual financial performance versus the forecast to uncover areas of strength and possible deviations that need to be adjusted.

## Step 2: Selecting Appropriate Forecasting Techniques

Depending on your goals and company stage, different forecasting methodologies provide differing degrees of complexity and applicability. Here are a few well-liked choices:

- Sales forecasting: is the process of estimating future sales using market trends, historical data, and industry growth estimates.

- Expense Forecast: Calculating your ongoing costs of operations, such as rent, supplies, marketing, and payroll.
- Cash Flow Forecast: Forecasting your cash input and outflow can help you make sure you have enough money to pay for bills and fulfill other commitments.
- Break-Even Analysis: This method tells you how profitable you are by calculating the point at which your sales income equals all of your costs.

## Step 3: Gathering Necessary Information and Presumptions

You must compile pertinent information and make reasonable assumptions about the many variables that may affect your finances in order to provide an accurate prediction. Among them are:

- Historical Data: Use your current business data, such as sales numbers and costs, to set your estimates' starting point.
- Market research: To learn more about possible consumer behavior and price tactics, examine industry publications, competition statistics, and market trends.
- Financial Assumptions: Make logical guesses regarding variables that might impact your company, such as interest rates, inflation, and general economic circumstances.

- Cost Estimates: Compute the expenses related to employment, marketing, production, and other operational facets of your company.

## Step 4: Building Your Financial Statements

Three essential financial statements comprise the fundamental elements of a financial forecast:

- Income Statement: This shows your anticipated profit or loss by projecting your income and costs over a given time period.
- Balance sheet: This shows your assets, liabilities, and shareholder equity and gives a quick overview of your company's financial situation at a particular moment in time.
- A cash flow statement: It shows how much money comes in and goes out of your company, letting you know if you have enough to run your operations and pay your debts.

## Step 5: Utilizing Financial Tools and Software

Spreadsheets are a useful tool for creating financial forecasts, but there are other software and financial tool possibilities as well. These can give visual representations of your financial plans, automate computations, and streamline data analysis.

## Step 6: Remember, It's a Dynamic Process

A financial projection is not a set, unchanging document. It's a dynamic tool that has to be routinely updated and examined. Be ready to modify your prediction as needed to keep it accurate and up to date when your company grows, the market shifts, and unforeseen events happen.

## Extra Advice:

- Develop multiple scenarios: Create a variety of scenarios to evaluate the robustness of your business model in a range of situations. You might want to consider forecasting based on different assumptions.
- Seek expert advice: If you need help developing a solid and precise financial projection, speak with accountants or financial consultants.
- Communicate effectively: Effective communication requires that your financial prediction be given succinctly and simply so that partners, investors, and other stakeholders may easily grasp your estimates.

You may arm yourself with a valuable tool that directs your company decisions, builds confidence in your endeavor, and lays the groundwork for assuring future success by developing a clear and flexible financial projection. Recall that the financial forecast is more than simply figures; it's about comprehending the financial narrative of your company and applying that understanding to successfully travel the thrilling but demanding path of entrepreneurship.

# Developing a marketing plan

The foundation of your entrepreneurial journey, your business plan serves as a road map for success. The marketing strategy is your compass in this important document, helping you to reach your target audience and, eventually, accomplish your business objectives. Your product or service is given life by the strategic story, which also generates curiosity and turns on potential consumers into devoted brand ambassadors.

How then can you create an effective marketing strategy that connects with your target market and drives the expansion of your business? We're about to go into the realm of marketing strategies and methods, so fasten your seatbelt!

**Step 1: Get to the Core of the Issue by Understanding Your Audience**
It's critical to have a laser-like understanding of your target demographic before you launch your marketing campaign. This

entails looking beyond demographics and exploring the core of your target audience's identity, desires, and requirements as met by your product.

Here are some important things to think about:
- Demographics: An essential foundation is provided by age, gender, income, location, and educational attainment.
- Psychographics: Online behavior, values, interests, personality traits, and lifestyle decisions provide a more in-depth understanding of an individual's preferences and motives.
- Needs and Pain Points: What goals, difficulties, and obstacles do they face? In what ways does your offering address these?
- Purchasing Routines: How do they investigate and make purchases of goods or services? Which advertisements and media appeal to them the most?

By using social media listening, interviews, and surveys to do market research, you may obtain priceless insights into your target market. It's important to keep in mind that knowing your target is a continuous process that guarantees the relevance and effectiveness of your marketing initiatives.

**Step 2: Clarifying Your Objectives and Setting Your Goals**

Once you are aware of your target market, establish specific, quantifiable marketing objectives. These objectives serve as your marketing journey's compass, ensuring that your efforts stay concentrated and in line with your overarching company goals.

Here are some crucial things to remember:

- Make sure your objectives are Time-bound, Relevant, Specific, Measurable, and Achievable (SMART) goals. With the help of this framework, you may monitor your development and evaluate the success of your marketing initiatives.
- Align with Business Objectives: Your marketing strategies should directly advance and aid in achieving your company's larger goals, which may include raising brand recognition, boosting revenue, or cultivating a devoted clientele.
- Put an emphasis on key metrics: Establish key performance indicators (KPIs) to monitor your advancement toward your marketing objectives. These might be metrics like conversion rates, social media interaction, website traffic, or client acquisition expenses.

## Step 3: Utilizing the Strategic Toolkit to Select Your Marketing Mix

Known colloquially as the "4Ps," the marketing mix consists of the fundamental components that form your marketing strategy:

- Product: Clearly state how your offering meets the demands of your target audience and what makes it stand out from the competition.
- Price: Choose a price plan that strikes a balance between market competitiveness, profitability, and your consumers' perception of value.
- Place: Decide which distribution channels—online, offline, or a combination of both—will work best for reaching your target audience.
- Promotion: Craft innovative content and persuasive messaging that connect with your audience and inspire them to take action.

## Step 4: Crafting Engaging Content – The Power of Storytelling

In the cluttered digital world of today, content is king. This includes a range of forms, such as:

- Blog entries: Provide insightful analysis, instruct readers, and position oneself as a thought leader in the field.

- Social media content: To engage your audience on relevant channels, use fascinating tales, interactive components, and eye-catching pictures.
- Email marketing: Use targeted email campaigns to generate prospects, establish rapport, and increase conversions.
- Video content: Use eye-catching video forms to draw viewers in, show off your good or service in action, and distribute testimonials.

Remember that your content should be educational and interesting, adding value to your audience's life by addressing their problems and providing answers. It shouldn't be just commercial in nature.

## Step 5: Learning and Adapting by Leveraging the Power of Measurement and Analysis

Marketing is a continuous process- what is effective one day may not be the next. As a result, track and evaluate the effectiveness of your marketing initiatives on a regular basis.

Here's how:

- Track your KPIs: To evaluate your success and pinpoint areas for development, keep an eye on the key

performance indicators you established for your marketing objectives.
- Make use of analytics tools: To obtain a better understanding of audience behavior and campaign efficacy, make use of email campaign metrics, social media insights, and website analytics.
- A/B testing: Determine which iterations of your marketing tactics—such as landing page layout or ad copy—resonate more with your target audience by trying them out.

You may focus your marketing efforts and deploy resources more effectively by examining your data.

# Chapter 4

*Bootstrapping Your Business: Building Your Dreams from the Ground Up*

Although the entrepreneurial spirit is strong, success is not always guaranteed by a smooth path. Obtaining finance is frequently the first obstacle for many would-be business entrepreneurs. While financing and investors might be very important, starting and expanding your business on your own, or bootstrapping, can be a profitable and practical option.

Being a bootstrapped individual involves not just being thrifty but also being creative, resilient, and resourceful. It involves creating your company piece by piece with calculated risks, your own creativity, and labor-intensive capital.

**Why Choose Bootstrapping?**

Although outside capital may provide a quicker route to expansion, bootstrapping has its own benefits:
- Retaining Control: You continue to be in charge of your company, making all of the important choices and holding complete ownership of it.

- Building a Solid Foundation: Starting a business on your own requires resourcefulness and efficiency, which promotes an innovative and lean operating culture.
- Increased Value: A bootstrapped company with a track record and a loyal client base attracts investors more readily when you finally go for investment.
- Developing Self-Reliance: The struggles and successes of bootstrapping provide your company a culture of pride, self-reliance, and ownership.

## The Essential Strategies for the Bootstrapper's Toolkit

You've made the decision to embark on the bootstrapping adventure. The following are some essential tactics to help you succeed:

- Begin Lean: Determine your MVP, or minimum viable product, which is a rudimentary version of your service that has just enough functionality to elicit insightful user feedback and verify your company idea. Prioritize developing and refining using data from the real world before expanding.
- Adopt ingenuity: Look into affordable options for anything from workplace space and equipment to marketing and technology. Whenever feasible, think about trading services, making use of open-source software, and making use of free internet resources.

- Become a Master of Sales and Marketing: Become an expert in sales and marketing by honing your techniques in order to draw clients and create income on their own. Make the most of every marketing dollar you spend by reaching your target audience via the use of social media platforms, content marketing, and strategic alliances.
- Cultivate Strong Customer Relationships: It's critical to give your customers outstanding service and to establish a solid rapport with them. This creates favorable word-of-mouth recommendations, repeat business, and loyalty—all of which are essential for long-term success.
- Seek Alternative Funding choices: Although the main idea is to minimize external funding, consider other choices such as microlending loans for small businesses or crowdsourcing. These can provide your company the much-needed boost without requiring you to give up a lot of control.

**Bootstrapping: A Journey of Growth and Learning**
There are obstacles on the path of bootstrapping. It calls for self-control, tenacity, and an openness to learning from errors. However, the benefits are significant. Throughout your entrepreneurial journey, you will benefit greatly from the skills you acquire, the resilient and resourceful culture you cultivate, and the solid foundation upon which you build your firm.

Here are some more reminders to keep in mind:

- Network strategically: Make strategic connections with mentors, industry experts, and other bootstrapped firms to acquire useful insights and learn from their experiences.
- Adopt a growth mentality and never stop learning and changing. Always look for new ways to grow, investigate cutting-edge technology, and modify your plans in response to consumer and market changes.
- Celebrate your victories: Give your accomplishments, no matter how modest, due attention and celebration. This will help you stay inspired and committed to your long-term objectives.

Note that the goal of bootstrapping is to create a solid basis for a lasting firm, not only to save money. Accept the difficulties, acknowledge the successes, and relish the process of building something genuinely amazing from the bottom up.

## Revealing the Finance Scene: Applying for loans or grants

Your inner entrepreneurial spark shines brightly, guiding you onward. After devoting all of your time and energy to creating an engaging business plan, the time has come to secure the capital needed to realize your dream. While bootstrapping provides a route to self-sufficiency, looking into loans and grants might quicken your progress and supply the funds need to realize your goals.

Getting Around the Financing Maze: Loans vs. Grants

Prior to getting started, it is important to comprehend the primary distinctions between loans and grants:
- Loans: A loan is simply a sum of money that you borrow from a lender and have to pay back over a certain amount of time with interest. There are legal ramifications for not repaying because this is a contractual requirement.
- Grants: A grant is an amount of money awarded that is not repayable. Grants, however, frequently have precise guidelines on the use of the money as well as reporting obligations.

**Examining the Financing Environment: Choices for Future Entrepreneurs**

There are several types of loans, and each has its own rules for qualifying, interest rates, and terms of repayment:

- Loans from the Small Business Administration (SBA): The SBA provides a range of loan programs that are especially intended for small enterprises, frequently with advantageous terms and interest rates. These loans may be used for a number of things, such beginning a business, growing it, or buying equipment.
- Term loans: These loans have a predetermined payback period and are perfect for covering certain one-time costs like buying equipment or funding home improvements.
- Line of Credit: This provides revolving credit up to a certain maximum, much like a credit card for your company. This can be useful in paying for recurring costs or unforeseen deficits.

**Obtaining a Loan: Preparing Yourself for Success**

Be sure you're ready to boost your chances of getting a loan:
- Create a Strong Business Plan: Your business plan is your road map, outlining the feasibility of your venture, your projected financial position, and your expansion strategy. This is how lenders determine the risk of giving you a loan.
- Develop a Strong Credit Score: Securing favorable loan conditions is dependent on having a solid personal and company credit score. Keep up a respectable credit history and, if needed, try to raise your credit score.

- Compile the Necessary Documentation: A variety of papers, such as tax returns, business licenses, and financial statements, may be required, depending on the kind of loan.

**The Granting Opportunity: Funding for Specific Objectives**

Grants are a strong option for funding acquisition, although they are frequently more competitive and have certain requirements:

- Government Grants: A number of government organizations provide funding for a range of objectives, including community development, environmental projects, and technical advancement. Look into grants that fit your business's aims and ambitions.
- Non-Profit Grants: A lot of non-profit organizations provide grants to companies that share their goals, which may include advancing social justice or encouraging innovation. Examine the grant programs offered by pertinent non-profit organizations.
- Grants from private foundations: These organizations occasionally provide funding to companies operating in their fields of interest. Make sure your company fits with the goals and financial objectives of any possible foundations by doing some research on them.

## Creating an Appealing Proposal to Win the Grant Game

In order to be noticed in the crowded grant market, create an engaging proposal that highlights the following:

- Clear Need: Clearly state the issue your company is trying to solve as well as the benefits it will provide.
- Solution & Strategy: Explain your suggested course of action and the best way to carry it out, highlighting how it meets the stated requirement.
- Financial Plan: Provide a thorough financial plan that explains how the grant money will be spent and how it will help you reach your goals.
- Team Expertise: Emphasize your team's experience and skills to show that they are qualified to carry out your suggested strategy successfully.

Note that applying for grants and loans involves careful planning, diligence, and study. Be ready to compete, and if you don't succeed in your first tries, don't give up. Your chances of obtaining the capital you want to support your entrepreneurial endeavors will rise if you are persistent and have a solid awareness of the requirements of lenders and the grant application procedure.

## Looking Beyond Grants and Loans: Investigating Other Options

Even while grants and loans are excellent sources of money, think about additional methods to diversify your funding sources:

- Crowdfunding: You may raise money directly from the public through websites like Kickstarter and Indiegogo in return for gifts, pre-orders, or shares in your company.
- Angel Investors: Affluent people who make investments in startups can offer capital as well as insightful guidance. Angel investors are prepared to assume greater risk in exchange for possibly large profits, therefore they frequently look for business with strong growth potential. Attend industry events, network with entrepreneurs, establish connections with angel investors, and make use of internet platforms that facilitate the introduction of businesses to possible investors.
- Venture Capital: Venture capital firms invest in high-growth companies that have the potential to generate large profits by pooling assets from many sources. They usually put their money into companies that have previously shown promise and need more capital to grow. Getting venture capital investment is frequently a difficult process that calls for a solid team, a well-developed business plan, and an inspiring future vision for your business.

## The Last Word: Picking the Correct Course

There are several possibilities available in the financial landscape, each having pros and cons of its own. The best course of action frequently combines several different tactics. While choosing which funding choices are ideal for your business, carefully assess your unique needs, financial objectives, and risk tolerance.

Remember that developing relationships is just as important as having enough money to secure sponsorship. Lenders and investors become participants in your journey, and building trusting connections with them is about more than just getting money. Show off your enthusiasm, devotion, and hard work for your company to build trust and enduring relationships that support your growth.

You may greatly improve your chances of obtaining the capital required to realize your entrepreneurial aspirations by thoroughly considering all of your choices, developing persuasive proposals, and putting together a clear business plan. Recall that obtaining finance is a process that calls for persistence, but with the appropriate strategy and steadfast commitment, you may turn your idea into a successful business.

# Crowdfunding Your Entrepreneurial Dreams

Although the entrepreneurial spirit is unquenchable, it sometimes takes a financial spark to realize your ambition. Aspiring business owners may find it intimidating to pursue traditional funding sources like loans or venture capital, which makes them uncertain about what to do next. This is where crowdsourcing steps in to revolutionize the game by providing a fun and democratic way to get money for your creative ideas.

**Demystifying Crowdfunding: Unleashing the Collective Power**
Through crowdfunding websites like Kickstarter, Indiegogo, and GoFundMe, a large number of potential funders (backers) may interact with individuals seeking financing (creators). When creators start a campaign, they introduce their concepts, goods, or initiatives and explain how they want to use the money. Subsequently, supporters provide their backing, sometimes in return for incentives, prizes, or even shares in the business.

**The Crowdfunding Environment: A Robust Ecosystem**

The crowdfunding ecosystem supports a wide variety of initiatives and companies, including:

- Creative projects: To generate money for their projects, singers, authors, filmmakers, and artists use crowdsourcing. They frequently provide special incentives like autographed copies, first access to their works, or exclusive artwork.
- Innovative products: Business owners use crowdsourcing to introduce items that are novel, giving supporters the opportunity to pre-order and receive discounts, turning them into early adopters and brand evangelists.
- Social issues: Crowdfunding is a tool used by individuals and nonprofit groups to generate money for a range of social causes. This helps them get the support of the community and promote awareness of their projects.

## The Allure of Crowdfunding: Benefits for Future Business Owners

For would-be business owners, crowdfunding offers a number of strong benefits:

- Accessibility: Crowdfunding is more accessible than traditional financing sources. It opens possibilities for those who lack substantial company history or collateral to receive money and eliminates geographical constraints.
- Feedback and Validation: Crowdfunding initiatives serve as a real-time instrument for market validation. The amount

of support you receive shows how interested the audience is in your concept and offers insightful criticism that will help you improve your good or service.
- Building Community: Having conversations with your backers helps create a feeling of community for your cause. Before you even launch, early adopters become your greatest evangelists, spreading the word and building a devoted following of clients.
- Flexibility: Funding choices through crowdfunding are flexible. Even if you don't raise the whole amount, you can still establish a financing goal and keep any money earned. This enables you to obtain important resources with even tiny contributions.

## Setting the Path: Launching a Successful Crowdfunding Campaign

It takes meticulous preparation and execution to turn your idea of crowdsourcing become a reality. Here are some crucial tactics to think about:
- Develop a Compelling Story: Write a compelling narrative that highlights your enthusiasm, the issue you address, and the benefits your initiative will provide. Make an emotional connection with your audience to entice them to join you on your trip.

- Set Realistic Goals: Look at related projects and decide on reasonable financial targets. This keeps you from setting yourself up for failure and shows that you understand the market.
- Provide Attractive benefits: Encourage backers to donate by offering them intriguing and valuable benefits. This might be first dibs on your goods, first access to items, or even project-related activities.
- Accept the Power of Marketing: To reach your target audience, make use of a variety of marketing methods. To promote your campaign, make use of social media, create an email list, and interact with relevant communities.
- Engage and Communicate: Throughout the campaign, be in constant communication with your supporters. Tell them how you're doing, answer any questions they may have, and thank them for their support.

## Beyond the Finish Line: Building Momentum after Crowdfunding

Having a successful crowdsourcing campaign is only the first step. It's important to keep the momentum you've created and fulfill your pledges to your supporters.

- Fulfill your commitments: Keep your word and provide your backers with the promised incentives on schedule.

This increases confidence and enhances the perception of your brand.
- Maintain communication: Even after the campaign is over, stay in touch with your supporters. Give them progress reports, offer noteworthy news, and extend an invitation to join you on your continuing adventure.
- Leverage the community: Make use of the community you have established during your campaign by leveraging it. Promote user-generated material, engage people on social media, and look for ways to communicate with your fans.

## Crowdfunding: An Important First Step in Your Entrepreneurship Career

For those who aspire to be entrepreneurs, crowdfunding has enormous potential. It may serve as a springboard for your business aspirations by cleverly utilizing its community-building capabilities, accessibility, and real-time feedback.

Always put in mind that the secret is to captivate your audience, establish trust, and present an entertaining tale. Crowdfunding may help you realize your vision and bring your original concept to life provided you put in the necessary effort, are creative, and have a well-planned campaign.

# Chapter 5

*Selecting the Right Business Structure for Your Entrepreneurial Journey*

You experience an awakening of your entrepreneurial spirit and your dream of a successful company materializes. You've given your all to creating an engaging business plan, obtaining capital, and are now prepared to take on the thrilling process of formally launching your enterprise. However, you must make one very important decision before you launch for company: selecting the best business structure.

It doesn't have to be scary to go through this seemingly complicated procedure. By being aware of the salient features and ramifications of different possibilities, you can arm yourself with the information necessary to make a well-informed choice that will assure your success.

**Unveiling the Options: A Glimpse into Common Business Structures**

A variety of legal structures are available in the business world, each with its own set of benefits and drawbacks.

- Sole Proprietorship: The simplest and most typical type of company structure is the sole proprietorship, in which the business is owned and run by only one person.
- Partnership: When two or more people join forces to co-own and run a firm, they divide earnings and losses in accordance with predetermined guidelines. There are mostly two kinds:
    - General Partnership: In a general partnership, each partner is fully liable for the debts and liabilities of the company.
    - Limited Partnership: General partners have unlimited responsibility, but at least one partner (usually the limited partner who invests but does not actively operate the firm) has limited liability.
- Limited Liability Company (LLC): Provides a hybrid form that combines a corporation's limited liability protection with the adaptability of a partnership. Limited liability protects LLC members' (owners') personal assets from obligations and liabilities incurred by the firm.
- Corporation: A separate legal entity from the people who own its shares. provides the best liability protection, but

comes with more complicated rules and procedures. There are basically two kinds:

- C Corporation: The most typical kind, liable to double taxation; shareholders pay taxes on dividends received, and the corporation pays taxes on its earnings.
- S Corporation: A smaller business that satisfies certain IRS requirements may choose to adopt pass-through taxation, in which earnings and losses are passed through to shareholders directly and recorded on their individual tax returns rather than the corporation paying income tax.

## Weighing the Factors to Choose the Correct Armor

Selecting the best organizational structure for a corporation necessitates carefully weighing several factors:

- Liability: To what extent are you willing to assume personal financial risk? Corporations provide the highest level of liability protection, while sole proprietorships and general partnerships provide the least.
- Management and Control: In a partnership or company, are you willing to share decision-making authority with others, or do you like to have complete control?

- Taxation: It's important to comprehend how each structure will affect your taxes. While corporations usually pay corporate income tax, partnerships and sole proprietorships pay taxes on their personal income tax filings.
- Formalities and Regulations: Certain organizational forms, such as companies, have more intricate record-keeping, meeting, and reporting requirements.
- Growth Potential: Take into account your long-range goals. A corporation can be a preferable option if you foresee considerable development and the need to obtain funds.

## Seeking Direction: A Supportive Hand on Your Path

Selecting the appropriate business structure is an important first step, and getting expert advice may be very helpful. To further understand the legal and tax ramifications of each choice and choose which structure best suits your requirements and objectives, think about speaking with a lawyer, accountant, or business counselor.

## Above and Beyond the Basics: Additional Things to Consider

Note that selecting a business structure is an ongoing process. Your demands may alter as your business develops. In the event that your company's ownership, operations, or development trajectory shift significantly, be ready to review your original choice and seek professional advice.

## The Last Word: Choosing the Framework that Strengthens Your Vision

Your basis for pursuing your entrepreneurial goals is the business structure you select. You may make an informed decision that supports your goal and propels your company towards success by thoroughly assessing your needs, consulting an expert, and keeping up to date.

Remember that picking the appropriate "armor" is about more than simply protection; it's also about deciding on the framework that will allow you to move, adjust, and prosper in the fast-paced world of business. Thus, go out on your adventure with assurance, knowing that the appropriate framework is waiting to assist you in turning your aspirations into a prosperous reality.

## Bringing Your Idea to Life: Registering Your Business with the Government

Your vision for a successful firm begins to take shape as your entrepreneurial spirit dances inside of you. Now that you have a solid strategy and the money to support it, you can start making your goal come true. However, there is still an essential step to do before you greet clients and start for business: registering your business with the government.

Although it may appear like a difficult administrative roadblock, this is a crucial step that certifies your business as a legal organization, enabling you to conduct business lawfully and enjoy a number of advantages. It's easier to navigate the registration process if you know the key processes and things to look out for.

**Demystifying the Procedure: A Step-by-Step Guide**
Depending on your area and the company form you have selected (sole proprietorship, partnership, LLC, or corporation), there are differences in the registration procedure. But the fundamental phases of the procedure are these generic ones:

**1. Select a Name for Your Business:**

- To make sure your preferred name is accessible and meets with state laws, do a name search.
- If the name under which your firm works differs from your legal name, you may want to register a "Doing Business As" (DBA) name.

## 2. Acquire the Required Licenses and Permits:

- Find out which licenses and permissions are necessary for the region and industry you operate in. These might include zoning permissions, business licenses, occupational licenses, and environmental or health permits.
- To get the required documents and information, get in touch with your state's licensing authorities or local government offices.

## 3. Put Legal Documents in Order:

- Sole Proprietorships: Generally speaking, no official state registration is necessary. But it can be required to register a DBA name or get particular permits.
- Partnerships: In certain states, filing a partnership agreement with the state may be required.
- LLCs: Submit your state's Secretary of State or a comparable office with your Articles of Organization. This agreement outlines the ownership and fundamental structure of the LLC.
- Corporations: provide your state's Secretary of State's Articles of Incorporation. This charter describes the goals

of the organization, as well as its original officers and directors.

## 4. Get an EIN, or federal tax identification number:

- A Federal Employer Identification Number, or EIN, is required for a number of activities, such as recruiting staff, creating a company bank account, and submitting federal taxes. The IRS website offers a free online EIN application process.

## 5. Register for State Taxes:

- You may be required to register for state income tax, sales tax, or other state-specific taxes, depending on where you live. For information on registration requirements, get in touch with the Department of Revenue in your state or a comparable organization.

**Above and Beyond the Basics: Additional Things to Consider**
Remember that registering your company is only the first step. Here are a few more things to remember:
- Requirements for Compliance: Remain informed about any current license, permit, or tax registration filing dates and requirements.

- Business Bank Account: To keep your personal and corporate funds apart, open a different type of bank account. In addition to streamlining recordkeeping and making tax filing easier, this gives your company financial legitimacy.
- Insurance: To safeguard yourself against potential hazards like property damage, liability claims, or employee injuries, think about getting company insurance.

## Seeking Advice: Seek the Assistance of Experts

Although this material gives a broad perspective, expert assistance can be helpful in understanding the complexities of business registration. Think about speaking with a:

- Lawyer: To help with the legal parts of registration, such as selecting a business structure, creating legal documentation, and making sure rules are followed.
- Accountant: For advice on tax consequences, establishing an accounting system, and comprehending the obligations for submitting state and federal taxes.

## The Last Word: Unlocking the Door to Success

Although it may seem like a difficult procedure, registering your company with the government is an essential first step that opens doors to legality, compliance, and other advantages. You may take the registration process with confidence and clarity if you know what to do, know when to seek expert advice, and keep yourself updated.

Keep in mind that your entrepreneurial adventure officially began with this registration. Remember that the foundation you lay now will support your progress and enable you to realize your entrepreneurial dreams as you further explore the world of business.

## Getting Through the Maze: Obtaining the Necessary Licenses and Permits for Your Business

You experience an inner spark of entrepreneurship that turns your idea into a workable strategy. You've picked a business structure, obtained finance, and filed your business registration with the government. You're now prepared to greet clients by opening your doors. To guarantee that your company runs lawfully and stays out of trouble, you must first get the required licenses and permissions.

**Deciphering the Permit Procedure: Understanding the Landscape**
Although the world of licenses and permissions might appear to be a complicated maze, you can effectively traverse it with a

little knowledge and preparation. What you should know is as follows:

- License vs. Permit: Although the terms are frequently used synonymously, licenses usually allow a business to continue doing a certain activity, whereas permits are usually project-specific and allow construction or other specialized activities.
- Federal vs. State vs. Local: Federal, state, and local government organizations may grant licenses and permits to you based on the nature of your business and its location.
- Industry-particular Requirements: Depending on your industry and region, a variety of particular licenses and permissions may be needed. For example, a construction business may require building permits and licenses for specialized professions like plumbing or electrical work, while a restaurant may require a food license, a liquor license, and a health inspection permit.

## Choosing Your Path: A Step-by-Step Guide

To properly navigate the licensing and permitting procedure, do the following actions:

**1. Investigate Your Needs:**

To find out what licenses and permissions are required for your particular business kind and location, start by contacting your local government agency (city or county). To assist you in determining your requirements, a number of government websites provide searchable databases or online tools.
- Professional associations or industry associations may also be excellent tools for learning about requirements unique to a given business.

## 2. Acquire the Required Applications and Forms:
- After determining which licenses and permissions are needed, get the application forms from the appropriate issuing organizations. Usually, the agency's office or its website have these forms.

## 3. Get the supporting documentation ready:
- You may be required to provide a number of papers, depending on the license or permission, including:
    - Documents used for business registration, such as DBA registration and articles of organization
    - Proof of insurance
    - Financial statements or business plans
    - Blueprints or floor layouts for building projects
    - Background checks or fingerprints (for some professions)

4. **Pay Any Relevant Fees:**
   - There are often costs connected with each license and permission. Don't forget to account for these costs when creating your budget.
5. **Submit Your Application and Await Approval:**
   - Before sending the applications to the appropriate organizations, make sure you carefully fill them out and acquire all necessary paperwork. Give yourself enough time to process and approve.

## Beyond the Basics: Extra Points to Think About

- Renewing a license or permission might be necessary for a number of reasons. To prevent functioning without proper permissions, set up reminders or make use of the online facilities provided by the granting agencies.
- Inspections: Regulatory bodies may conduct recurring inspections of you, depending on your industry. Make sure your company abides by all laws and upholds the necessary safety standards.
- Modifications to Operations: Take note of any additional license or permit requirements that may apply if you grow your company or relocate.

## Seeking Advice: Getting Expert Assistance

It may be difficult to navigate the complicated world of licenses and permissions, particularly for new business owners. Think about contacting:
- Consultants or advisers for businesses: They may help you with applications, lead you through the procedure, and determine whether you require a license.
- Professionals in the field: Make contact with people in your industry who are able to provide their knowledge and insights on pertinent license and permit needs.
- Lawyers that focus on business law: They may offer legal counsel on particular licensing matters and guarantee that your company complies with all relevant rules.

**The Last Word: Unlocking Growth and Compliance**
Getting the required licenses and permissions may appear like one more obstacle, but doing so is essential to become legally compliant and, eventually, growing your business. Through comprehension of the procedure, comprehensive investigation, and assistance when required, one may confidently maneuver through the labyrinth of licenses and permissions, guaranteeing seamless operation of their firm and setting the stage for sustained prosperity.

Remember that acquiring the required licenses and permissions shows your dedication to professionalism, safety, and moral business conduct in addition to satisfying legal obligations. So set out on this trip with the understanding that every step you take will improve your foundation and provide you the tools you need to create a successful and ethical business.

# Chapter 6

*Create a Marketing Plan and Build Your Brand: Establishing Your Brand in a Competitive Environment*

For an entrepreneur to succeed in the ever-changing modern economy, distinctiveness is essential. Even if a well-designed product or service is a crucial starting point, creating a unique and captivating brand identity takes your business from being a simple entity to a potent force for expansion and connection.

**Analyzing the Core: Revealing the Influence of Brand Identity**
Your brand identity goes beyond simple graphics, such as slogans and logos. It captures the essence of your company, including your personality, beliefs, goal, and the special promise you provide to your target market. It creates an emotional bond and shapes a certain impression in their thoughts, which is the core of how they will remember and interact with your business.

**Why Invest in Defining Your Brand Identity?**

Beyond only helping with looks, having a clear brand identity has several advantages:
- Clarity and Focus: It ensures consistent message across all touchpoints and acts as a strategic roadmap for your marketing and communication initiatives.
- Competitive Differentiation: It distinguishes you from other businesses, allowing you to carve out a special niche for yourself in the industry and draw in your target clientele.
- Customer Connection: It creates an emotional bond with your target audience and builds a feeling of community while cultivating a sense of trust and loyalty.
- Employee Engagement: A compelling brand identity motivates and unites staff members by assisting them in realizing their part in realizing the company's goals and creating a feeling of common purpose.

**Building a Brand Identity: A Methodical Approach**
Establishing your brand identity requires thought and initiative. This is a road map to help you along the way:

**1. Discovering Your Essence:**
- Begin by reflecting about yourself. Determine the mission statement and guiding principles of your company. Which core beliefs serve as the foundation for your decision-

making? What issue are you trying to solve, and what kind of difference do you want to make?
- Identify your target market by carrying out in-depth market research to learn about their requirements, desires, goals, and current brand preferences.

## 2. Creating a Story for Your Brand:
- Create an engaging tale that narrates the history of your brand. What is the narrative of your birth? How have you overcame obstacles? What distinguishes you from rivals?
- Put your personality and ideals into your tale. What distinguishes your brand from others? Which tone of voice would you want to employ when speaking? Make sure your target audience can relate to and find authenticity in your tale.

## 3. How to Visualize Your Brand:
- Create a polished brand design and logo that embodies your company's identity. Select fonts, colors, and images that express your ideals and appeal to your target market.
- Ensure visual coherence on all platforms, including your packaging, marketing materials, and social media accounts in addition to your website.

## 4. Authentically Living Your Brand:

- Your brand identity should be present in every engagement you have with clients, including those through your website and customer support.
- Make sure your behaviors align with the principles you value by acting with authenticity and consistency in all of your communications.

## Going Above and Beyond: Considerations for a Robust Brand Identity

- Competitive Analysis: Learn about and comprehend the brand identities of your rivals. Find ways to set yourself apart from the competition and present a special value proposition.
- Market Research: Keep a close eye on your target audience's changing tastes, perceptions, and reactions to various branding components by doing continuing market research.
- Changing Over Time: Your brand identity may and should change to keep up with market trends and maintain relevance with your target audience, even if your underlying principles stay the same.

## Seeking Advice: Working Together for Success

Creating a brand identity definition may be a challenging and rewarding task. Think about working with the following experts:

- Marketing consultants and branding agencies: They may offer professional advice, carry out in-depth market analysis, and assist you in creating a thorough brand plan.
- Graphic designers: They are capable of creating a visually striking brand identity that complements your narrative and appeals to your target market.
- Copywriters and messaging specialists: They can assist you in creating communication materials and brand messaging that successfully communicate your company's distinctive voice and value proposition.

**Unleashing a Unique Brand's Power**

Developing your brand identity is a strategic investment in the future of your company, not merely an aesthetic process. You build difference, connection, and long-term growth by accepting this process. Recall that having a clear brand identity gives you the ability to connect intimately, speak truthfully, and cultivate a following of devoted clients who share your values and vision.

## Developing Effective Marketing Strategies to Propel Your Brand

You've created an engaging brand identity that is a colorful tapestry made of your goals, beliefs, and distinctive tale. The important work of creating marketing tactics to advance your brand, engage with your target market, and build lasting relationships now begins.

## Getting Around the Marketing Landscape: A Multidimensional Strategy

A wide range of strategies are included in marketing, all of which are intended to accomplish particular goals. The following are some vital strategies to consider:

- Content Marketing: Information marketing is the process of producing and disseminating interesting, educational, and useful information in a variety of media (blogs, articles, films, infographics), with the goal of drawing readers in, establishing your credibility, and building trust.
- Search Engine Optimization (SEO): By making your content and website more visible in search engine results, you can make sure that potential clients will find your business when they look for relevant keywords.
- Social Media Marketing: Connect with your audience, tell the story of your company, and create a community around your products and values by using social media sites like Facebook, Instagram, and LinkedIn.

- Email marketing: Create an email list and send tailored, educational, and interesting emails to nurture leads, advertise your goods and services, and forge closer bonds with your clients.
- Public relations and influencer marketing: To expand your audience and raise brand exposure, team up with relevant influencers or media sources.
- Paid Advertising: Target certain audiences with well designed paid advertisements to increase website traffic, produce leads, or advertise particular goods or services. You may do this by using platforms like Google Ads or social network advertising.

## Customizing the Approach: Aligning with Your Goals and Resources

Several elements determine the best marketing plan for your business:

- Who is the audience you are aiming to reach? Selecting the best communication channels requires an understanding of their interests, demographics, and internet habits.
- Your Business Goals: Do you want to raise revenue, create leads, improve website traffic, or raise brand awareness? Establishing your objectives helps you choose the most effective marketing techniques.

- Your Resources: When selecting marketing strategies, take into account your team size, budget, and skill sets that are available. As you gain experience, start with tactics you can carry out well and increase them.

**Creating a Successful Strategy: 5 Key Steps**
1. Identify your target market, the competitive environment, and the most recent marketing trends by conducting market research.
2. Establish precise, quantifiable targets to monitor the effectiveness of your marketing initiatives (e.g., lead generation rate, growth in website traffic).
3. Select the appropriate marketing channels: Match the behavior of your target market and your company's objectives with the channels you've selected.
4. Provide valuable material that is in line with your business identity, speaks to your audience, and is visually appealing.
5. Measure, evaluate, and adapt: Keep a close eye on the effectiveness of your marketing initiatives, evaluate the data, and modify your plans as necessary to get the best possible outcomes.

**Going Above and Above: Making the Most of Your Marketing Plan**

- Develop a personalized customer experience: Create a customized customer experience by addressing each individual client in your marketing communications and interactions to build greater ties and loyalty.
- Embrace storytelling: Tell stories in your marketing campaigns to emotionally engage your target audience and increase brand recall.
- Remain flexible and adaptable: Be ready to modify your marketing plans in response to consumer input, rivalry, and market developments.

**Seeking Advice: Working Together for Successful Marketing**
It might be difficult to create and carry out a good marketing plan. Think about working with the following experts:
- Marketing consultants: They can help you create a thorough marketing plan that is in line with company objectives and financial constraints. They can also offer strategic advice.
- Digital marketing experts: They can assist you in efficiently reaching your target audience by utilizing a variety of digital marketing channels, such as SEO, social media marketing, and email marketing.
- Content creators: They can help you create interesting and captivating material that connects with your readers and produces outcomes.

**The Last Word: Harnessing Strategic Marketing's Power**
Creating successful marketing tactics involves more than simply advertising your goods or services—it also entails establishing deep relationships with your target market. Understanding your market, matching your tactics to your objectives, and encouraging teamwork can help you transform your compelling brand identity into a powerful tool that drives recognition, client acquisition, and long-term success.

Remember that developing a strong brand involves constant iteration and adjustment. With a strategic mindset, a dedication to education, and the understanding that each step you take on your marketing journey will get you one step closer to realizing your entrepreneurial goals, embrace this trip.

# Weaving the Web: Orchestrating Online and Offline Marketing Channels for Brand Harmony

Building your brand requires a symphony of online and offline channels in the ever-changing world of marketing. With their own advantages and scope, every channel presents a chance to establish significant connections with your intended audience. You can establish a unified and powerful brand experience that is consistent throughout all touchpoints by balancing these channels.

**The Digital Stage: Unveiling the Power of Online Channels**
Our lives are now completely dependent on the internet, and there are many different ways to engage with your audience through online channels:

- Website: Your website acts as your online headquarters, offering useful information and presenting your brand's narrative together with your offerings. Make sure it is informative, easy to use, and search engine optimized.
- Search Engine Optimization (SEO): Make sure your online presence and content are optimized for search engines to help your website rank higher. This will ensure that potential customers will find your brand when they are looking for relevant keywords.
- Content Marketing: Create and share valuable, informative, and engaging content in various formats (blogs, articles, videos, infographics) to attract and engage your audience, establish yourself as an authority in your field, and nurture trust.
- Social media marketing: It involves connecting with your audience through sites like Facebook, Instagram, or LinkedIn, sharing your brand narrative, creating a community around your products and ideals, and running

targeted ads to appeal to particular interests and demographics.
- Email marketing: Create an email list and send personalized, educational, and interesting emails to nurture leads, advertise your goods and services, forge closer bonds with clients, and encourage brand loyalty.

## The Physical World: Leveraging the Potential of Non-Online Channels

Even if the digital world has a ton of promise, offline channels may still be quite important for creating connections and increasing brand awareness:
- Attend trade exhibitions, conferences, or industry events to network with influencers, partners, and possible customers.
- Public relations and influencer marketing: To expand your audience and raise brand exposure, team up with relevant influencers or media sources.
- Print advertising: To reach a specific audience and present your brand's message, use publications that are related to your industry or local newspapers.
- Promotional events and sponsorships: To raise brand awareness and establish a personal connection with your

target audience, take part in neighborhood gatherings, volunteer projects, or sponsor pertinent events.
- Brochures, flyers, and printed materials: Use superior printed materials to exhibit your company, goods, or services at trade exhibitions, events, or physical venues where your target market visits.

## Bringing the Whole Symphony Together: Fostering Coherence Through All Media

Creating a cohesive and consistent brand experience via the coordination of online and physical channels is the key to unleashing the full potential of marketing. This is how to bring about this harmony:
- Keep your brand identity constant by making sure that your visual identity, voice, and messaging are reflected in all of your marketing materials, whether they are printed or distributed online.
- Employ cross-channel marketing: Make use of the influence of several channels to spread the word about your message. On your website, highlight your social media handles; utilize email marketing to direct visitors to certain landing pages; or host offline events to promote online interaction.

- Track and analyze: Keep an eye on the results of your offline and online marketing initiatives to see what connects with your target demographic and modify your approach accordingly.

## Beyond the Basics: Making the Most of Your Multi-Channel Strategy

- Leverage the power of data: Make the most of your data by using analytics tools to learn about the behavior of your customers on various channels and tailor your marketing appropriately.
- Adopt experiential marketing: To strengthen emotional ties and increase brand loyalty, provide your audience with interesting and interactive experiences both online and off.
- Analyze the impact of offline channels: Although calculating the return on investment (ROI) of offline marketing may not be as simple as it is for online channels, get inventive and devise strategies to evaluate the success of your offline initiatives in relation to your particular objectives (e.g., foot traffic increase at an event, coupon redemption rates).

## Seeking Direction: Collaborating for Orchestral Success

Effective marketing symphonies need to be orchestrated with skill and cooperation. Think about collaborating with the following experts:

- Marketing consultants: They may offer strategic direction for creating a thorough marketing strategy that smoothly combines offline and internet media.
- Experts in digital marketing: From website creation and search engine optimization to social media and email marketing, they can assist you in making the most of online platforms.
- Public relations experts: They can help you establish connections with influencers and media sources to increase your brand's visibility and awareness.

**The Last Word: Putting on a Perfect Show**

Through a strategic integration of online and offline channels, you can effectively craft a memorable brand experience that appeals to your target audience at every touchpoint.

# Chapter 7

*From Vision to Validation: Creating Prototypes and Minimum Viable Products (MVPs)*

The entrepreneurial path depends heavily on creativity and in-depth knowledge of client demands. After you've conceived of an appealing product or service, the next critical phase of development is about to begin. Creating prototypes, also known as Minimum Viable Products, or MVPs, is a common first step in this stage. These are concrete representations of your idea that open the door to testing, validation, and, eventually, a successful product launch.

**Differentiating the Ideas: Prototypes vs. MVPs**

Prototypes and MVPs, although frequently used synonymously, have different functions in the development process:
- Prototypes: A physical versions of products or services, frequently in the early stages of development. Their intricacy can vary, ranging from simple drawings to more sophisticated, functioning prototypes that are more like

the finished item. Their main objective is to evaluate form, function, and usability; this way, before you commit substantial resources to development, you may get user input and make iterations to your design.
- Minimum Viable Products (MVPs): MVPs are working products with the essential functionality required to support your main market hypotheses. In contrast to prototypes, which are mostly utilized for internal testing, MVPs are introduced to a small group of users in order to obtain feedback from actual users and confirm the value proposition of the product.

**Advantages of Prototyping and MVPs:**

- Reduced Risk: Before spending a lot of money on development, you may find any problems and improve your product by testing frequently and early.
- Enhanced User Focus: By gathering insightful user input, prototypes and MVPs help you make sure your solution fulfills a genuine market need.
- Better Resource Allocation: You may allocate resources more wisely and steer clear of expensive development errors by iterating based on early feedback.

- Enhanced Efficiency: By letting you concentrate on the most important features and functions first, prototyping and MVPs help speed up the development process.

**Creating Your Prototype: A Step-by-Step Guide**

1. Establish Your Objectives: What are your learning objectives for this prototype? Is the purpose of testing the user interface, functionality, or general user experience?
2. Select the Appropriate Degree of Fidelity: Take into Account the Product's Complexity and Development Stage. For early testing, begin with low-fidelity prototypes (like as drawings or paper prototypes) and move up to higher quality prototypes (such interactive prototypes) if necessary.
3. Create Your Prototype: Apply a range of instruments and methods according to the degree of realism you have selected. This might be drawing, using software to create mockups, or using easily accessible materials to make basic, non-functional prototypes.
4. Conduct Testing: Ask prospective consumers for their opinions through usability testing, interviews, or A/B testing, which compares several prototype iterations.

**Factors to Take Into Account for Successful Prototyping**

- Quick Iteration: Be ready to make adjustments to your prototype in response to user input. Creating a product that genuinely connects with your target market requires this iterative approach.
- Cost-Effectiveness: Especially in the early phases, keep your prototypes basic and economical. Getting early input is more important than producing a polished end result.
- Align with Your MVP: For consistency in user experience and feedback gathering, make sure your prototype is in line with the features you intend to include in your MVP.

**Creating Your MVP: Launching the Learning Experiment**

1. Determine Your Core Value Proposition: For your target market, what is the primary issue that your product or service resolves?
2. Establish the MVP Feature Set by ranking the elements that are most important to proving the value proposition to your target market and validating your main hypothesis.
3. Develop the MVP: Keep development time and resource allocation to a minimum and concentrate on creating a working product with essential features.
4. Launch Your MVP: Make your MVP available to a select number of early adopters. Use a variety of methods (such as surveys, interviews, and user testing) to get input in

order to confirm your market assumptions and get insight into their experience.

**Factors to Take Into Account for a Successful MVP**
- Pay Attention to User Experience: An MVP should provide a pleasant and easy-to-use interface even with its limited feature set.
- Be Open and Honest with Users: Make it obvious that you are releasing an MVP and are looking for input to help you make the product better.
- Measure and Learn: Monitor important performance indicators like user engagement, conversion rates, and use statistics to find out what works and what needs improvement for your audience.

# Finding Reliable Suppliers and Vendors for Your Business

An concept has taken off, your brand identity is clear, and your marketing plan is set up. The critical process of creating and sourcing your goods or services is about to begin. You need dependable vendors and suppliers who can supply the necessary supplies, time, and knowledge to make your idea a reality if you want to see your vision come to life.

## Getting Around the Supplier Landscape: Understanding the Participants

The realm of vendors and suppliers comprises a heterogeneous array of entities, each of whom assumes distinct functions within the supply chain:
- Manufacturers: Businesses that create the raw ingredients or completed products you need.
- Wholesalers are companies that buy goods in large quantities from producers and then resale them to companies much like yours.
- Distributors: Organizations that handle shipping and logistics in between manufacturers and retailers.
- Service Providers: Organizations that supply specialized services necessary for running your business, such web developers, marketing agency, and logistical suppliers.

## Finding the Correct Partners: Important Things to Keep in Mind
Selecting the appropriate vendors and suppliers involves carefully weighing several aspects, including:

- Quality: Make sure the goods or services you get live up to your expectations and represent your brand.
- Reliability: Select partners that have a track record of reliably fulfilling requirements and delivering work on schedule.
- Cost: Get comparative quotations and bargain fairly, taking into account the value proposition as a whole rather than simply the upfront cost.
- Communication and Customer Service: Look for partners that will answer your questions promptly, communicate clearly, and deliver top-notch customer service.
- Ethical Considerations: Select partners that share your commitment to sustainability and commercial ethics.

**Finding the Perfect Match: A Step-by-Step Guide**
- Define Your Needs: Clearly state what goods or services you require, along with the features and quantity you would want.
- Investigate Possible Suppliers: To find possible partners, visit trade exhibitions, industry magazines, or use internet directories.
- Get Proposals and estimates: Get in touch with the suppliers you've narrowed down your list of options, and ask them for comprehensive estimates that include the

cost, lead times, conditions of payment, and service level agreements (SLAs).
- Evaluate and Compare: Examine the bids you have been given, contrast prices, gauge the caliber of the goods and services being provided, and gauge each supplier's professionalism and communication.
- Finalize and Negotiate Agreements: Work with your selected provider to create a mutually advantageous deal by negotiating terms and price.

**Beyond the Basics: Building Strong Supplier Relationships**
While locating trustworthy suppliers is essential, developing solid, cooperative partnerships is just as vital. Here are some pointers:
- Keep lines of communication open: To promote openness and trust, be sure to convey your requirements, expectations, and any potential obstacles on a regular basis.
- Develop a relationship of trust and respect by being mindful of your suppliers' contributions to your company's success.
- Make sure to pay your payments on time. This shows that you are a professional and improves your connection with your partners.

- Consider long-term partnerships: Establishing enduring bonds with dependable providers may result in reduced expenses, enhanced correspondence, and increased dependability.

**Seeking Advice: Working Together for Successful Sourcing**

Several experts' knowledge can be useful in navigating the challenges of sourcing:
- Business consultants: They may provide advice on sourcing wisely, negotiating contracts, and identifying acceptable suppliers.
- Industry experts: Make connections with people in your field to learn about trustworthy vendors and suggested procedures.
- Experts in sourcing: They can help you find possible partners, carry out in-depth market research, and negotiate advantageous terms.

**The Last Word: Harnessing the Potential of Trustworthy Vendors**

One of the most important steps in turning your idea into a successful business is locating and establishing a rapport with trustworthy suppliers. You may set the stage for reliable product quality, effective operations, and long-term success by knowing the market, doing extensive research, and carefully vetting possible partners. Recall that your suppliers are partners who are essential to the success of your company, not just providers. Strong, win-win partnerships can help you maintain a dependable supply chain and position yourself to provide outstanding value to your clients.

## Ensuring Quality Control in Your Products or Services

Gaining and keeping the trust of customers is crucial in the dynamic corporate world. One most important thing determines this trust: quality. Whether you sell real goods or intangible services, what makes you stand out from the competitors and promotes long-term success is maintaining a consistently high standard of quality.

**Deciphering the Environment: Understanding Quality Control**
The methods used to keep your goods and services at the appropriate caliber are collectively referred to as quality control, or QC. It is a proactive strategy that reduces risk and guarantees a consistent and satisfying customer experience by

spotting and resolving possible problems before they affect your clients.

**The Benefits of Effective Quality Control:**
- Increased Customer Satisfaction: Reliability fosters trust and happiness, which attracts repeat business and effective word-of-mouth advertising.
- Decreased Costs: By reducing waste, rework, and product returns, proactive quality control methods can help you save money over time.
- Better Brand Reputation: Standing out from the competition and continuously providing high-quality goods or services enhances your brand image.
- Operational Efficiency: Production efficiency may be increased and operations can run more smoothly with streamlined quality control procedures.

**Implementing a Robust Quality Control System: A Step-by-Step Guide**

1. Establish Your Quality Standards: Using thorough specifications, performance benchmarks, or service level agreements (SLAs), clearly state the quality level you expect for your goods and services.

2. Determine Critical Control Points (CCPs): Mark the crucial phases of your manufacturing or service delivery process where possible problems with quality might occur.
3. Apply Control Measures: Apply a range of control measures, such as the following, in accordance with the identified CCPs:
    - Inspection of incoming materials: Before using, make sure that any raw materials or components match your quality requirements.
    - In-process inspections: To find and fix possible problems early on, do inspections at different phases of production.
    - Final product inspection: Before a product is sent, make sure it complies with all standards by conducting comprehensive inspections.
    - Service quality checks: Put in place systems for observing and assessing the provision of services to make sure they adhere to your established criteria.
4. Establish Documentation and Record-keeping: Keep thorough records of your quality control methods, inspection findings, and any remedial measures you took to resolve any problems.
5. Conduct Regular Audits: To evaluate the performance of your quality control system and pinpoint areas for development, conduct internal audits.

## Beyond the Basics: Factors to Take Into Account for Efficient Quality Control

- Adopt a Continuous Improvement Mindset: Based on data analysis and input from internal teams and customers, continuously look for methods to enhance and optimize your quality control procedures.
- Invest in Technology: To automate data gathering, optimize workflows, and enable real-time production or service delivery monitoring, use quality control software or tools.
- Empower Your Team: Develop a culture of quality inside your company by providing training on quality control processes and giving your staff the freedom to see and report possible problems.

## Seeking Advice: Working Together for High-Quality Success

The following professions' knowledge might be useful for implementing a strong quality control system:

- Professionals in quality control: They can help you with audits, data analysis, and development and implementation of quality control methods.
- Industrial engineers: They can find economical solutions to improve quality control procedures and assist you optimize your manufacturing operations.

- Consultants for quality assurance: They may provide advice on establishing and managing an extensive quality management system (QMS) that complies with global standards such as ISO 9001.

**The Last Word: Unleashing the Potential of Superior Quality**
Putting money into quality control helps your company create an excellent culture rather than merely ensuring that minimal requirements are met. A proactive and all-encompassing strategy can help you guarantee a steady stream of high-quality products and outstanding service, which will eventually build the groundwork for a successful and long-lasting company. Recall that quality is an ongoing process of improvement that calls for devotion, teamwork, and a desire to going above and beyond for customers.

# Chapter 8

*Launch Your Business and Start Selling: Setting your launch date and creating a buzz*

The birth of your firm and the beginning of your path to success mark the climax of your entrepreneurial journey, and it is almost here. Choosing the best launch date and creating pre-launch hype are two essential components of this phase that guarantee a fruitful and memorable debut.

**Selecting Your Launch Date: Important Strategic Factors**
Choosing the best launch date is a calculated risk that can have a big effect on your company's performance. The following are crucial points to consider:

- Market Seasonality: Is there a particular season or period of the year that usually sees a rise in demand for your item or service? Try to time your launch to take advantage of this seasonality.
- Competitive Landscape: Take into account your rivals' launch dates and steer clear of directly conflicting with significant product launches or advertising campaigns.

- Internal Preparation: Make sure your company is ready to manage the surge of prospective clients brought on by the launch. This entails having a capable staff, an adequate inventory, and a strong customer support system.
- External Factors: Keep in mind that there may be outside influences on your launch, such as vacations, significant occasions, or prevailing economic conditions.

**Creating Pre-Launch Buzz: Sparking Excitement**

A successful launch involves building anticipation and enthusiasm among your target audience before you ever open your doors, in addition to having a fantastic product or service. The following are some successful pre-launch buzz-generating techniques:

- Create an Engaging Brand Story: Tell compelling tales that accentuate your beliefs, mission, and distinctive selling point to tell your brand's story.
- Leverage Social Media: Make use of the many social media channels to communicate with your audience, reveal early looks at your goods or services, and create buzz by doing freebies, competitions, or interactive surveys.
- Build an Email List: To nurture prospects, share progress reports on your launch, and provide unique pre-launch discounts or early access chances, create an email list and publish interesting newsletters.

- Influencer marketing and public relations: Collaborate with relevant media sources or influencers to reach a larger audience and produce favorable press coverage or reviews prior to your debut.
- Make a Landing Page: Create a landing page just for your launch, provide clear information about it, encourage email sign-ups to generate leads, and create excitement about what's to come.
- Collaborate with Complementary Businesses: To create buzz for your launch and to promote each other's products and services, collaborate with companies that cater to the same target market as you.

## Beyond the Basics: Maximizing Your Pre-Launch Efforts

- Create a feeling of community: Encourage user-generated content, hold online competitions centered around your goods or services, and interact with your followers on social media platforms in order to create a feeling of community around your business.
- Leverage the power of visuals: To draw attention and present your offering in an appealing manner, make use of eye-catching images, such as enticing product photographs, interesting films, or eye-catching graphics.
- Run targeted online advertising: Raise awareness and spark interest in advance of your launch by utilizing

internet advertising channels to reach your particular target group.

**The Day of Launch and Beyond:**

On the momentous day, remember to:

- Perform flawlessly: Make sure your customer support channels are accessible and responsive, your website is operating as intended, and your staff is ready to take orders or queries.
- Track and analyze: Keep an eye on your website traffic, sales figures, and marketing initiatives to see what connects with your target market and modify your approach appropriately.
- Nurture relationships: Create enduring bonds with your clients by going above and beyond their expectations, offering first-rate customer service, and encouraging loyalty via constant interaction.

**Seeking Advice: Collaborating for a Successful Launch**
Several professions' knowledge can be useful in navigating the launch process:
- Marketing consultants: They can help you with managing your internet presence, producing impactful marketing materials, and formulating a thorough pre-launch plan.

- Public relations experts: They can assist you in gaining media attention and cultivating connections with writers and opinion leaders who can promote your business.
- Launch specialists: These experts may provide knowledge and experience in organizing different parts of your launch, guaranteeing a seamless and prosperous debut.

**The Last Word: Planning an Amazing Debut**

Starting a business is an exciting event that signifies the start of your entrepreneurial adventure. You may spark enthusiasm, grab attention, and create the conditions for long-lasting and significant success by strategically choosing your launch date and creating pre-launch buzz using innovative and captivating marketing techniques. Recall that creating good customer connections and consistently surpassing expectations is what lays the groundwork for long-term development, not just the early excitement that accompanies a successful launch. So, seize the moment, harness the strength of teamwork, and propel your company into an exciting future.

## Implementing Your Marketing Plan for Launch Success

Your marketing strategy, which outlines the ideas and techniques to drive your firm towards success, has been painstakingly prepared. The critical next step is to put those plans into action. The link between your clearly stated strategy and the observable outcomes you aim to attain is effective execution.

**The Pillars of Effective Marketing Plan Implementation:**
1. Setting SMART Goals: Make sure your marketing objectives are Time-bound, Relevant, Specific, Measurable, and Achievable (SMART) before launching into action. This clarity helps you stay on course, monitor your progress, and make any modifications.
2. Assigning Roles and Responsibilities: Clearly state who is in charge of each marketing strategy component. Assign work according to each person's skills and areas of strength to guarantee effective completion.
3. Creating a material Calendar: Make a detailed schedule that details the material you will produce and distribute across different media. This keeps you organized, guarantees consistency, and supports your entire marketing objectives.
4. Using Technologies and Tools for Marketing: To maximize your campaigns, assess campaign effectiveness, and streamline your efforts, make use of analytics software, social media scheduling systems, and marketing automation tools.

# Launching Your Marketing Machine: Strategies in Action

## 1. Marketing using Content:

- Publish top-notch content: Make insightful, interesting, and worthwhile information that is in line with the requirements and interests of your target audience.
- Make use of a variety of information formats: To accommodate varying learning styles and preferences, try blog posts, infographics, videos, podcasts, or e-books.
- Effectively promote your content by extending its reach through influencer relationships, email marketing, and social media.

## 2. Marketing on Social Media:

- Establish a strong social media presence: Build a solid social media presence by making profiles on pertinent sites and modifying your material to fit the audience and structure of each platform.
- Engage with your audience: Interact with your audience by holding interactive surveys or

competitions, swiftly answering messages and comments, and taking part in pertinent discussions.
- Utilize paid advertising: To reach a larger audience and accomplish particular campaign goals, think about using targeted social media advertising.

## 3. Email Marketing:

- Develop your email list: Providing worthwhile incentives (like discounts or access to special content) to entice people to join up.
- Audience segmentation: It involves adjusting your email content to each segment's unique demands and interests.
- Customize your emails: Use the names of your subscribers and tailoring the content to suit their interests or previous exchanges.

## 4. Search Engine Optimization (SEO):

- Optimize your website: To raise its position in search engine results pages (SERPs), make use of pertinent keywords, excellent content, and sound technical SEO techniques.

- Build backlinks: Create backlinks to your website by obtaining links from trustworthy websites, which shows search engines that your website is an important resource.

**Maximizing Your Marketing Initiatives**
- Adopt a data-driven decision-making process by employing analytics tools to track the effectiveness of your marketing campaigns on a regular basis. Examine important indicators to determine what is succeeding and what need improvement, such as website traffic, engagement rates, conversion rates, and return on investment (ROI).
- Test and refine: Don't be scared to try out various marketing approaches and techniques. To find out what appeals to your audience the most, A/B test several iterations of your content, calls to action, or advertising campaigns.
- Keep up with the newest tools, technology, and trends in marketing to remain ahead of the curve and modify your strategy accordingly.

**Seeking Advice: Working Together for Successful Marketing**
Seeking the advice of several experts can help you execute your marketing plan more successfully:

- Digital marketing specialists: They can help with email marketing campaigns, social media management, content production, and search engine optimization.
- Content marketing specialists: They can assist you with creating a thorough content strategy, producing interesting material in a variety of formats, and successfully distributing it through numerous channels.
- Analytics specialists: They can help you with data interpretation, tool setup, and insight generation to improve the success of your marketing efforts.

**The Last Word: Marketing is a Journey, Not a Destination**
Remember that effective marketing is a continual process that involves implementation, observation, modification, and improvement. Through a combination of strategic planning, data-driven decision making, efficient execution, and flexibility, you can turn your marketing strategy from a guide into a potent tool that drives your company's long-term success.

# Making your first sales: Strategies and Tactics to Secure Your Initial Customers

A journey of a thousand miles begins with a single step, applies to business, where that initial step is equivalent to closing your first deal. This apparently small gesture has great significance since it starts your business journey and signals the shift from desire to validation.

## Laying the Foundation: Creating a Sales-Ready Base

Prior to implementing sales strategies, make sure your company is prepared to turn leads into customers:

- Improve your value proposition: By outlining the special benefits your product or service provides and how it addresses the particular issues faced by your target market.
- Develop a compelling sales pitch: Create a succinct, powerful message that highlights the advantages of your service and connects with the audience to create a strong sales pitch.
- Price your products or services competitively: Set rates that are both lucrative for your company and appealing to your target market by conducting in-depth market research to learn what your competitors are charging.
- Create a clear sales process: By outlining the phases in your sales cycle, from generating leads to completing deals.

**Techniques to Get Your First Sales:**

1. Utilize your network: Make contact with the people in your current circle of friends, family, coworkers, and acquaintances. Give them a tour of your business concept, outline the value proposition, and provide incentives to become your initial clients.
2. Make use of online marketplaces: Depending on your offering, you might want to list it on sites like Etsy, Amazon, or Fiverr. By doing this, you may reach a larger audience and access a more diverse consumer base.
3. Engage in cold outreach by determining the profiles of your ideal clients and use email marketing, social media messaging, or cold calling to reach out to them specifically. Tailor your strategy, emphasize how your product or service relates to their requirements, and provide helpful information or advice.
4. Provide free trials or demos: By providing free trials, demos, or consultations, you may let prospective clients see the worth of your good or service for themselves. This might boost their confidence and encourage them to buy anything.
5. Run promotional campaigns: To encourage early adopters and create initial sales momentum, think about providing exclusive discounts, bundles, or early-bird access.
6. Engage in industry events: Go to conferences, trade exhibits, or networking gatherings that are pertinent to

your sector. This gives you the opportunity to present your products, establish a connection with possible clients, and create leads.

**Beyond the Basics: Strategies for Effective Sales**

- Don't only concentrate on sealing the transaction; give equal importance to developing sincere connections with potential clients. Make an effort to actively hear their needs, respond to their worries, and position oneself as a reliable resource.
- Become an authority in your sector by keeping up with changes in the market, your industry, and the competition. This gives you the confidence to converse with potential clients and prove your knowledge.
- Accept the power of storytelling and incorporate engrossing tales into your sales presentation. Tell tales of how your good or service has assisted others in overcoming obstacles in order to emotionally engage potential clients.
- Develop your skills in addressing objections: Be ready to respond intelligently to any possible concerns from customers. Plan ahead for frequently asked questions, provide succinct, understandable answers, and highlight the benefits your business offers despite any apparent downsides.

- Never stop learning and improving your strategy: Examine your experiences with customers, determine what works and what doesn't, and keep improving your sales pitch, techniques, and overall plan.

## The First Sale's Significance and Beyond

Although getting your first sale is a big accomplishment, it's only the beginning. Every transaction supports expansion, verifies your company strategy, and yields insightful client feedback. As you move on, bear the following in mind:

- Treat every customer with respect and appreciation: No matter how little the transaction, every customer is important, so treat them with respect and gratitude. Exceed their expectations and establish enduring connections to promote great word-of-mouth advertising and repeat business.
- Never stop innovating and improving: since the business environment is ever-changing. Remain ahead of the curve by always assessing your products and services, seeing where you can make improvements, and adjusting to shifting consumer demands.
- Honor your achievements, but also learn from your failures: Be proud of what you've accomplished, but also evaluate the difficulties you've faced and the areas where

you still need to grow. Having a growth attitude can help you advance in your business endeavors.

## Seeking Advice: Working Together for Successful Sales

The following professionals' knowledge can help you improve your sales capabilities:

- Sales trainers: They can provide you the tools you need to handle objections, close transactions, and conduct productive sales interactions.
- Mentors in business: Skilled businesspeople may provide priceless advice and assistance, sharing their knowledge and assisting you in overcoming obstacles unique to your sector and market.
- Sales consultants: They are able to evaluate your current sales procedure, point out areas that need work, and make recommendations for tactics that will enhance your success and sales efforts.

# Chapter 9

*Keeping Accurate Financial Records for Business Success*

Knowing where you are financially is essential for success in the fast-paced world of business. This is the point at which keeping precise and thorough financial records is important. It serves as both the record of your company adventure and the compass that directs your decision-making. You may obtain the crucial insights required to optimize earnings, pinpoint opportunities for development, and guarantee the long-term sustainability of your endeavor by keeping a regular and precise financial record.

**Understanding the Importance of Accurate Financial Records:**

Keeping up-to-date financial records has several advantages:
- Making Well-Informed Decisions: Cash flow, profitability, costs, and revenue are all crucially tracked down in financial records. You may use this information to make well-informed decisions regarding pricing policies, the

distribution of resources, and the general course of your organization.
- Tax Compliance: To file proper tax returns and stay out of trouble with the law or fines, accurate records are necessary.
- Obtaining Funding: To evaluate the financial standing and future prospects of your company, prospective lenders and investors mostly rely on your financial records when making loan or investment requests.
- Finding Trends and Opportunities: You may take advantage of opportunities and foresee future difficulties by tracking patterns in your income and spending through the analysis of financial data collected over time.
- Peace of Mind: Focusing on expansion and strategic planning is made possible by knowing that your finances are in order. This gives you a sense of security and control over your company's activities.

## Constructing a Sturdy Accounting Recordkeeping System:
1. Choose a Bookkeeping Method: Depending on the size and complexity of your company, choose an appropriate accounting approach (such as cash accrual basis).
2. Invest in Bookkeeping Software: To make data input more efficient, automate computations, and produce financial

reports more quickly, think about using accounting software.
3. Categorize Transactions: To make analysis and reporting easier, clearly sort your revenue and outlays into standardized, consistent categories.
4. Reconcile Accounts Regularly: To maintain accuracy and spot any inconsistencies, reconcile your bank and credit card statements with your accounting records on a regular basis.
5. Maintain Appropriate Documentation: For future reference, keep all pertinent financial papers, including bank statements, invoices, and receipts, well-organized and easily accessible.

## Sustaining Economic Well-Being

- Set Financial Goals: Clearly define your company's financial objectives, such as hitting a target profit margin or growing sales by a given percentage. Regularly monitor your progress toward these objectives by using your financial information.
- Create Financial Forecasts: In order to prepare for growth and potential financial issues, create financial forecasts that anticipate future revenue and spending.
- Seek Professional Assistance: As your company expands, think about enlisting the help of a certified bookkeeper or

accountant. They can manage intricate financial duties, provide professional guidance, and guarantee that your records are correct and in compliance with legal requirements.

**Common Pitfalls and How to Avoid Them:**
- Combining personal and business funds: To prevent misunderstanding and possible legal problems, keep your personal and corporate finances completely apart.
- Ignoring recordkeeping: Don't put off doing your bookkeeping! Make sure your records appropriately represent your financial condition by updating them on a regular basis.
- Not being able to comprehend financial statements: In order to grasp the information they give, become familiar with the fundamental financial statements, such as the cash flow, balance, and income statements.
- Ignoring the effects on taxes: To guarantee correct tax filing, keep up with tax laws and deadlines. If necessary, don't be afraid to seek expert advice.

**Seeking Advice: Collaborating for Financial Achievement**

Keeping thorough financial records can be aided by the knowledge of several experts:

- Accountants: They are capable of providing a broad variety of services, such as assistance with bookkeeping, financial analysis, tax preparation and filing, and strategic financial planning.
- Bookkeepers: These experts are capable of handling regular reporting, data entry, and reconciliation among other bookkeeping duties.
- Financial advisors: They may offer comprehensive financial guidance, assisting you in managing the funds of your company, creating investment plans, and making well-informed decisions on your future finances.

**The Last Word: Taking a Financial Awareness Approach**
Maintaining accurate financial records requires more than just math—it also requires awareness, understanding, and management. Carefully keeping track of your finances gives you the ability to overcome obstacles, take advantage of chances, and eventually lead your company to long-term success. Recall that the key to every successful business endeavor is financial acumen.

# Analyzing Your Sales and Marketing Data for Growth

In the dynamic world of business, data is king. While creativity and intuition play a major role in the success of entrepreneurs, data-driven decision-making is the key to strategy optimization, resource optimization, and sustained development. This is where the analysis of marketing and sales data is useful. Examining the data will provide you with important information that will show you what is doing well, what needs to be improved, and finally, how to set yourself up for long-term success.

**Why Analyze Sales and Marketing Data?**

There are several advantages to studying sales and marketing data analysis:
- Find patterns and trends in your sales data: By identifying patterns in your sales data, such as seasonal variations or the success of particular marketing efforts, you may adjust your strategy as necessary.
- Measure marketing ROI: Determine which marketing strategies are producing the greatest results and make future investment decisions by measuring the return on investment (ROI) of your marketing efforts.
- Optimize customer acquisition costs: Determine the most economical methods to expand your marketing budget

and draw in new clients by doing a customer acquisition costs (CAC) analysis.
- Improve audience targeting: Boost audience targeting by learning more about the characteristics, interests, and habits of your customers. This will help you craft marketing messages that are more likely to be resonant with your target market.
- Forecast future sales: Use past sales data analysis to forecast future trends and schedule your production and inventories appropriately.

Crucial Measures for Marketing and Sales Analysis:

- **Sales Data:**
    - Total income
    - Sales by product or service
    - Customer acquisition cost (CAC)
    - Customer lifetime value (CLTV)
    - Average order value
- **Marketing Data:**
    - Website traffic
    - Conversion rates (e.g., website visitors to leads, leads to customers)
    - Cost per click (CPC)
    - Participation on social media

- Email marketing open rates and click-through rates (CTRs)

## Beyond the Numbers: Instruments and Methods for Efficient Analysis

- Use data visualization tools: Make use of tools like as dashboards, graphs, and charts to display data in an aesthetically pleasing and understandable way that makes trends simpler to see.
- Adopt data segmentation: To obtain a deeper understanding of distinct client categories and adjust your plans appropriately, divide your data according to demographics, past purchases, or other pertinent factors.
- Test several iterations of your marketing efforts (e.g., landing page designs, email subject lines) to determine which are most successful and to improve your strategy. This is known as A/B testing.
- Benchmark your performance: To evaluate your success and pinpoint areas for improvement, compare your metrics to those of the industry or to your own historical statistics.

## Beyond the Basics: Complex Techniques for Data-Driven Decision Making

- Predictive analytics: Make educated judgments regarding resource allocation, marketing campaigns, and product

development by using sophisticated data analytics technologies to forecast future consumer behavior.
- Map your customers' journeys from first awareness to purchase and after-purchase experiences to find possible obstacles and chances to raise customer happiness and retention.
- With the use of marketing attribution modeling, you can more efficiently assign credit and budget resources by identifying which marketing touchpoints—such as website visits, social media interactions, and emails—contribute most to conversions.

## Common Challenges and How to Overcome Them:
- Avoid trying to evaluate everything at once to avoid data overload. Prioritize critical indicators that are pertinent to your present objectives first.
- Limited data expertise: To aid with difficult data analysis and interpretation, think about hiring marketing consultants or data analysts as professionals.
- Problems with data quality: To prevent false insights, make sure your data is accurate by putting data quality tests and cleaning methods in place.
- Having trouble putting ideas into practice: Don't simply get information; do something with it! Based on your

research, create practical plans of action and monitor their success with continuous data analysis.

## Seeking Advice: Collaborating for Data-Driven Achievement

Utilizing the knowledge of many experts can help you fully unlock the value of your sales and marketing data:

- Data analysts: They can help with data collection, cleansing, and analysis. They can also spot important trends and provide tools for data visualization so that insights are presented in an easy-to-understand manner.
- Marketing consultants: They may help with data interpretation, the creation of data-driven marketing plans, and the optimization of your marketing initiatives to meet predetermined objectives.
- Experts in marketing automation: They can assist you with setting up the systems necessary to track campaign effectiveness, automate tedious operations, and extract insightful information from consumer data.

# Making Adjustments to Your Business Plan for Sustainable Growth

The one constant in the fast-paced world of business is change. Although a well-written business plan is an essential guide, it's important to keep in mind that it's not infallible. In order to maintain your plan's relevancy and take advantage of any unanticipated opportunities or obstacles that may present themselves along your entrepreneurial journey, you must make the necessary revisions.

Accepting the Need for Adjustment:

A company strategy that is adaptive and flexible enables you to:
- React to changes in the market: Modify your tactics in response to evolving consumer preferences, rivalry, or changes in the financial system.
- Profit from unanticipated opportunities: Take advantage of chances that don't quite work out as planned to take advantage of new market demands or technology developments.
- Learn from experience: Gather insightful information from actual data and client comments to help you make better decisions about your product or service offerings, costs, and marketing tactics.
- Preserve a competitive advantage: In a market that is always changing, you can stay ahead of the curve and

preserve a competitive edge by being adaptable and flexible in your approach.

Identifying When Changes Are Required:

There are a few indicators that your company strategy needs to be reviewed and perhaps adjusted:
- Not reaching predicted sales or revenue targets: If your real results show a big difference from your estimates, it's time to review your pricing strategy, target market, and sales and marketing tactics.
- Shifts in consumer behavior or preferences: To stay relevant and competitive, you may need to make adjustments to your product or service offerings, message, or marketing channels when customer demands and preferences change.
- New laws or regulations: Modifications to the legal environment or new rules may call for alterations to your company's operations or compliance protocols.
- Customer and partner feedback: Pay special attention to what customers, partners, and industry experts have to say. Their observations might highlight areas in need of development and offer chances for tactical changes.

Making Effective Adjustments to Your Business Plan:

1. Collect information and evaluate performance: To identify areas in which your strategy needs to be modified, evaluate market trends, consumer input, and key performance indicators (KPIs).
2. Determine the main issue or opportunity: Clearly state the problem you're trying to solve or the opportunity you want to take advantage of.
3. List possible fixes: Look into several ways to modify your strategy, taking into account their viability and possible effects.
4. Evaluate and choose the best approach: Determine the optimal course of action by weighing the possible outcomes of each choice and picking the one that best fits your resources and overarching business goals.
5. Update your plan and documentation: Make sure your team members are aware of any modifications and update your plan to reflect the agreed-upon alterations.
6. Track and monitor progress: Keep an eye on how well your updated strategy is working and make any necessary revisions going forward.

Beyond the Fundamentals: Approaches to Effective Adaptation
- Adopt a culture of continuous improvement: Encourage an environment in your company that is conducive to ongoing experimentation, learning, and adaptation.

- Make backup plans: Make backup plans to deal with unanticipated circumstances or possible obstacles so you can respond swiftly and effectively.
- Keep lines of communication open: Make sure all members of your team and stakeholders are aware of any changes made to the business plan so that everyone is on board with the updated approach.
- Seek outside counsel: If you need help managing complicated modifications, think about consulting seasoned business consultants or mentors who may provide insightful advise and encouragement.

Typical Mistakes and How to Prevent Them:
- Disregarding the need for change: Don't stick with antiquated tactics just because your strategy initially included them. Be open to changing as a result of fresh knowledge and market conditions.
- Absence of preparation and planning: Avoid making snap decisions without giving them much thought. Before making changes, consider all available choices, assess any potential repercussions, and make sure everyone is on board.
- Neglecting to communicate effectively: To prevent misunderstandings and guarantee that all parties are in

agreement with the updated strategy, clearly convey any changes to your team, stakeholders, and possible partners.

**The Last Word: Adapting to Change to Maintain Success**
An effective business plan is a dynamic, breathing document that serves as a roadmap for your entrepreneurial endeavors. As long as you accept that change is inevitable, keep a close eye on your development, and make the necessary modifications, your business plan will continue to be applicable, flexible, and ultimately, a driving force behind long-term success and growth. Recall that flexibility and adaptation are essential for overcoming obstacles, grasping opportunities, and long-term success in the fast-paced world of business.

# Chapter 10

*The Road to Success: Overcoming Common Challenges Faced by Small Businesses*

Starting and maintaining a small business is an exciting adventure with a wealth of benefits. It is, nonetheless, a journey not without its share of difficulties. Gaining insight into the typical obstacles that small businesses encounter will enable you to overcome them and improve your chances of success.

**Financial Management:**

- Limited access to capital: Getting finance for your company might be quite difficult. Investigate other possibilities such as raising funds from venture capitalists or angel investors, applying for loans from banks or credit unions, or bootstrapping.
- Cash flow management: Sustaining a positive cash flow is essential to the ongoing operations of a firm. Create a reliable budgeting system, keep close tabs on all spending,

and think about rewarding clients for early payments to speed up cash flow.
- Managing profitability: It requires a careful balance between income and costs. Consider pricing carefully, keep overhead under control, and always look for methods to increase your profit margins.

**Sales and Marketing:**

- Reaching your target audience: It might be difficult to pinpoint your ideal client and successfully communicate with them. To establish a connection with your audience, make use of social media, a variety of advertising platforms, and customized marketing techniques.
- Making a name for yourself: In a competitive market, setting your company apart from the competitors is essential. Emphasize customer service, highlight your special value offer, and cultivate a close rapport with your target market.
- Turning leads into sales: A clearly defined sales process is necessary to close the transaction and turn leads into devoted clients. Use persuasive communication techniques, provide them with solutions that are appealing, and persistently follow up with prospective clients.

**Operating Difficulties:**

- Wearing several hats: Running a small business requires you to handle a variety of tasks, from customer service to marketing. As much as feasible, assign work to others, use technology to automate procedures, and develop good prioritization skills.
- Time management: For any entrepreneur, time is a valuable resource. To keep organized and increase productivity, make a clear calendar, assign priorities to your work, and use time management tools.
- Maintaining compliance with regulations: It can be difficult to navigate the many legal and regulatory obligations. To make sure your company is operating in compliance, get expert help from attorneys or accountants.

**Building Your Team:**

- Identifying and recruiting talent: Hiring motivated, talented workers is essential to the expansion of any company. To draw and keep great personnel, build strong relationships, provide benefits and salary that are competitive, and create a happy work atmosphere.

- Trust and delegation: Develop your ability to assign work to others and have faith in your team to carry out their responsibilities. This gives you more time to concentrate on strategic choices and gives your team members a feeling of accountability and ownership.
- Managing a team: Successful team management requires excellent communication, teamwork, and the development of a pleasant work environment. Develop a culture of gratitude and acknowledgment, give frequent feedback, and make investments in the professional growth of your staff.

**Beyond the Obstacles: Extra Success Techniques**
- Adopt a growth mentality and never stop learning and changing. Keep abreast of market developments, pursue new education and training, and have an open mind to criticism and adjustment.
- Create a strong network: Connecting with other business owners, specialists in the field, and possible partners may offer invaluable opportunities, support, and insights.
- Honor and appreciate your accomplishments: Give due consideration to all of your accomplishments, no matter how minor. This maintains the motivation of your staff and cultivates a happy workplace.

Always remember that you are not alone. These are the kinds of obstacles that countless small enterprises must overcome, and the secret to their success is early planning, ongoing education, and flexibility. These typical obstacles may be avoided by being aware of them and arming yourself with the knowledge and techniques you need to overcome them, convert obstacles into opportunities, and clear the path to a flourishing business.

## Overcoming Obstacles: Strategies for Sustainable Business Growth

There is seldom a straight pathway to success in the business journey. You will inevitably run upon roadblocks, hurdles that will test your determination and require creative answers. But development and resilience frequently bloom in these times of adversity. Through the acquisition of effective tactics for surmounting difficulties, you may convert setbacks into opportunities for long-term, sustainable corporate success.

**Cultivating a Growth Mindset:**

- Have a "can-do" mentality: Encourage an optimistic and problem-solving outlook. Have faith in your abilities to overcome obstacles and approach problems by concentrating on coming up with workable solutions.
- Accept lifetime learning: Develop an inclination for lifelong learning. Actively look for ways to broaden your knowledge and skill set by going to industry workshops, reading pertinent articles, or asking mentors for advice.
- Reframe failures as teaching moments: See obstacles as chances for personal development. Determine the underlying source of the problem, draw insightful conclusions from the encounter, and make the necessary adjustments to avoid reoccurring problems.

**Developing Resourcefulness and Resilience:**
- Create a solid support system by surrounding yourself with upbeat, encouraging people who share your goal and provide encouragement. This network of support may be quite helpful in trying times, offering both practical and emotional support.
- Put self-care first: Keep a good work-life balance and give your physical and emotional health first priority. Take part in stress-reduction and relaxation exercises; a calm mind is better able to face obstacles and make wise choices.

- Use your imagination and ingenuity: Don't be scared to come up with novel solutions when presented with challenges. To get over the obstacle, think of inventive ideas, make efficient use of the resources at hand, and take into account several strategies.

**Strategic Planning and Execution:**
- Identify possible difficulties in advance: To foresee possible roadblocks, thoroughly analyze competitors and the industry. This enables you to create backup plans and lessen the effects of any unforeseen circumstances.
- Develop a flexible and adaptable business plan: Create a flexible and adaptive company strategy since an inflexible one would not be able to handle unanticipated difficulties. Make sure your company strategy is adaptable enough to handle last-minute changes and unforeseen circumstances while staying true to your overarching strategic goals.
- Focus on effective implementation: although having a well-defined plan is important, executing it well is much more so. Create well-defined action stages, assign responsibilities efficiently, and keep a careful eye on development to make sure your strategy produces observable outcomes.

**Seeking Direction and Cooperation:**

- Seek mentorship: Make connections with seasoned business owners or professionals in the field who can provide insightful advice and mentorship. Their knowledge, suggestions, and practical expertise may guide you through difficulties and steer clear of typical errors.
- Use professional services: To handle certain issues, think about using the assistance of knowledgeable specialists, such as attorneys, accountants, or marketing consultants. Their knowledge might reduce your burden and free you up to concentrate on your key skills.
- Create strategic alliances and partnerships: Collaborating with firms that complement one another may be advantageous for both parties as it enables you to take advantage of each other's assets and capabilities to overcome obstacles and accomplish common objectives.

**The Power of Perseverance: A Cornerstone of Success**

A necessary component of becoming an entrepreneur is facing challenges. Perseverance is the key to sustainable business success, even while excellent plans can provide you the means to traverse them. Recall that the most prosperous businesspeople are not those who shy away from difficulties but rather those who continually overcome them by demonstrating unflinching resolve and a dedication to growth and adjustment.

You may give yourself the skills to turn setbacks into learning opportunities and turn them into stepping stones toward long-term company success by adopting a growth mindset, developing resilience, putting strategic planning into practice, and actively seeking out cooperation. Recall that the path to business success is paved with both worthwhile lessons learned and successes. Accept the difficulties, grow from them, and let them mold you into a more capable businessperson.

## Crucial Tools for Successful Small Business Ventures

Owning a small business has both obstacles and opportunities. While enthusiasm and hard work are essential components, having access to priceless resources may greatly increase your chances of success. This last part outlines some of the most important tools at your disposal to support your business endeavors.

Government Resources:

- U.S. Small Business Administration (SBA): The SBA provides small companies with a wide range of resources and acts as a one-stop shop. These resources include:
    - Free business counseling: Get in touch with knowledgeable mentors who can offer advice on a range of business-related topics.
    - Business plan templates and guidelines: Create a thorough and well-thought-out business plan by using the SBA's tools.
    - Grants and loan programs: Look into several financial aid options to get money for your company endeavors.
- State and local government agencies: A lot of state and local governments provide extra resources that are especially designed for companies that fall under their purview. These might consist of:
    - Tax incentives: Find out what local small companies may be eligible for in terms of tax cuts or exemptions.
    - Training and development programs: Access training classes on business fundamentals including marketing, finance, and human resources. Participate in training and development initiatives.
    - Networking opportunities: Participate in government agency events and activities to make connections

with other local business professionals and entrepreneurs.

**Non-Profit Organizations:**

- SCORE: This nonprofit organization pairs seasoned mentors with startup companies to provide free, private business advice.
- Small Business Development Centers (SBDCs): A nationwide network of facilities that provide free or reasonably priced courses, training, and business advice.
- Industry-specific associations: A number of sectors have set up organizations that offer its members useful services including advocacy assistance, instructional materials, and networking opportunities.

Online Resources:

- SCORE website: Visit the SCORE website to have access to a plethora of free online resources covering a range of company management topics, such as webinars, templates, and articles.
- SBA website: Go through the SBA website to find out all the details about their services, programs, and online learning tools.

- Industry publications and websites: To keep informed about industry trends and best practices, subscribe to industry magazines or follow relevant blogs and websites.
- Online tutorials and courses: A wide range of websites provide inexpensive or even free tutorials and courses on a variety of business subjects, including digital marketing, finance, and marketing.

**Extra Sources:**

- Professional networks: Use local networking organizations or internet resources like LinkedIn to establish connections with other business professionals and entrepreneurs.
- Mentorship programs: Seek the advice of seasoned company executives who may provide invaluable direction and encouragement for your entrepreneurial endeavors.
- Books and podcasts: Dive into the world of entrepreneurship with enlightening reads and listens from knowledgeable and accomplished company executives and experts.

Remember that you are not alone yourself. Make use of the wide range of resources at your disposal to provide yourself the information, encouragement, and direction you need to successfully negotiate the opportunities and difficulties of operating your own business. You may improve your chances of creating an effective and long-lasting business by actively utilizing these tools and by learning and adjusting on a constant basis.

**Beyond Resources: The Power of Community**

Even while there are tools available to offer advice and support, the entrepreneurial journey is fundamentally a personal one. Developing a solid network of experts and small business owners may be a priceless asset in and of itself. You may build a feeling of community and gain insightful knowledge that will help you advance by talking about your experiences, supporting one another, and taking lessons from each other's triumphs and setbacks.

Accept the tools at your disposal, network with other business owners, and never forget that running a small business requires constant learning, adjustment, and development. With commitment, tenacity, and the appropriate resources at your disposal, you may make your business dream a prosperous reality.

www.ingramcontent.com/pod-product-compliance
Lightning Source LLC
Chambersburg PA
CBHW071053240526
45471CB00015B/1835